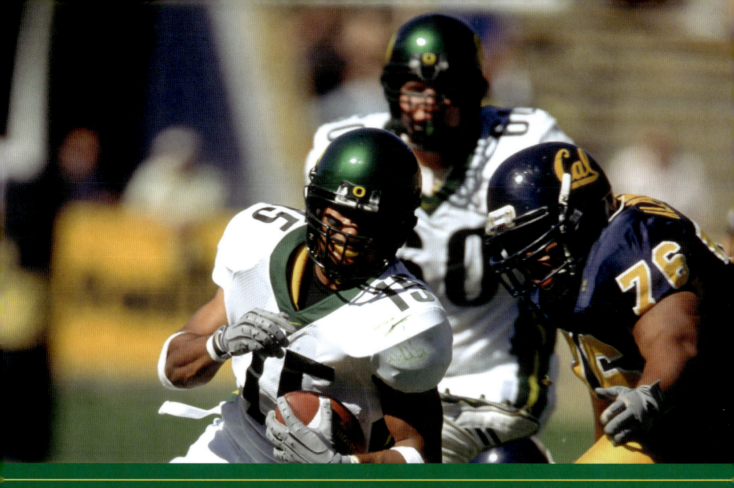

GAME DAY
OREGON FOOTBALL

GAME DAY
OREGON FOOTBALL

*The Greatest Games, Players, Coaches and Teams
in the Glorious Tradition of Duck Football*

TRIUMPH
BOOKS

Athlon® Sports™
AMERICA'S PREMIER SPORTS ANNUALS

Library of Congress Control Number: 2007902217

This book is available in quantity at special discounts for your group or organization. For further information, contact:

Triumph Books
542 South Dearborn Street
Suite 750
Chicago, Illinois 60605
(312) 939-3330
Fax (312) 663-3557

CONTRIBUTING WRITER: Rob Moseley

EDITOR: Rob Doster

PHOTO EDITOR: Tim Clark
ASSISTANT PHOTO EDITOR: Danny Murphy

DESIGN: Eileen Wagner
PRODUCTION: Patricia Frey

PHOTO CREDITS: Athlon Sports Archive, AP/Wide World Photos, University of Oregon

Printed in China

ISBN: 978-1-60078-017-2

Contents

Foreword

by Dan Fouts

I am a Duck. I know it is a rather silly nickname, but it is a "dam" sight better than being a Beaver! And it seems that in this great state of Oregon, you are one or the other.

What does it mean to me to be a Duck? Well, let me first tell you how I came to be a Duck. I grew up in San Francisco and played football at St. Ignatius High School. On our city championship team of 1967, 11 players received scholarship offers to play football in college. I was one of the lucky 11, but just barely.

While some of my teammates were weighing offers from a number of schools, I had but one choice—the University of Oregon was the only school to offer me a scholarship. Head coach Jerry Frei and his defensive backs coach George Seifert (whose recruiting area was the San Francisco Bay Area) saw enough potential in me to take the flyer. I will be forever grateful to Coach Frei for having the guts to extend the offer and then for having the faith in me to be his quarterback. To this day, I consider earning a full ride scholarship as one of my proudest accomplishments.

Pride is the word that comes to mind when I think about what it means to me to be a Duck. I am proud of my associations, acquaintances and friendships that were forged on the rain-soaked AstroTurf of Autzen Stadium. To me, what is more important than records or scores or statistics are the relationships that I made in my four years in Eugene. I am proud of having played in a football program that was built by the legendary Len Casanova and enhanced by one of the finest coaches and men I've known, Jerry Frei. It was a program that had integrity, class and the best interests of the student-athletes at its core.

Coach Frei surrounded himself with young coaches that went on to great honor and distinction. John Robinson was our offensive coordinator. He later was a Rose Bowl–winning coach at USC and eventually head man of the Los Angeles Rams. George Seifert went on to lead the San Francisco 49ers to Super Bowl glory. Our running backs coach, Bruce Snyder, coached the Arizona State Sun Devils to the Rose Bowl. Gunther Cunningham became a renowned defensive coordinator in the NFL, and John Marshall, after coaching my winless Oregon frosh team in 1969, has enjoyed success in the NFL as well. Perhaps if the Ducks had had a better quarterback in those days, they might have posted a better record. But, that is another story for another time.

The entire coaching staff made sure we as players were always prepared for anything and everything. We were not the deepest or most talented teams, but we always felt we were capable of winning each and every time we took the field. It is those times that I remember most. Standing in the huddle in the middle of the Los Angeles Coliseum trailing the UCLA Bruins by 19 with a little over four minutes to go; staring into the eyes of my center Jim Figoni and the rest of the offensive linemen; checking out the cool demeanor of receiver Greg "Chatsworth" Specht; and marveling at the incredible heart, desire, class and athletic ability of Bobby Moore (Ahmad Rashad) is just one of many wonderful memories that fill my thoughts when I think about being a Duck. Oh yeah, we won that game 41–40!

Now, to have *Game Day: Oregon Football* on my bookshelf affords me the opportunity to relive those great times and the chance to remember the glory days of Van Brocklin, Renfro, Berry, Wilcox, Harrington, Brooks, Bellotti and so many others.

But most importantly, it reminds me of how thankful I am for having been given the shot at playing football for the place that always feels like home to me—the University of Oregon. GO DUCKS!

Introduction

The images are unforgettable and too numerous to count.

Norm Van Brocklin, the "Flying Dutchman," striking fear into the Pac-10. A long line of talented successors at the quarterback position, from Dan Fouts to Bill Musgrave to Joey Harrington. An astounding selection of skill players, hard-nosed linemen and tough, aggressive defenders. The evolution of a cutting-edge image that has led college football into a new century. Some of the best facilities in all of college sports. A packed Autzen Stadium, giving full-throated support to its beloved Ducks. Championships won; legends created.

We're distilling the pageantry and drama of Oregon football into the pages that follow. It's a daunting task. Few college football programs in the country inspire the loyalty and passion that the Duck football program exacts from its fans—and with good reason.

The numbers alone are impressive: bowl appearances in 14 of the last 18 seasons, heading into 2007. Five former Ducks in the Pro Football Hall of Fame. Countless statistical milestones.

But numbers alone don't do justice to the greatness of Oregon football. The Duck program stands for something deeper, a true commitment to excellence in every phase.

Through the words and images we present, you'll get a taste of what Oregon football is all about. Decades have passed since players first donned the green and yellow, but one thing hasn't changed: Oregon football is an unmatched tradition, a legacy of greatness, a way of life.

Touchdown Ducks!

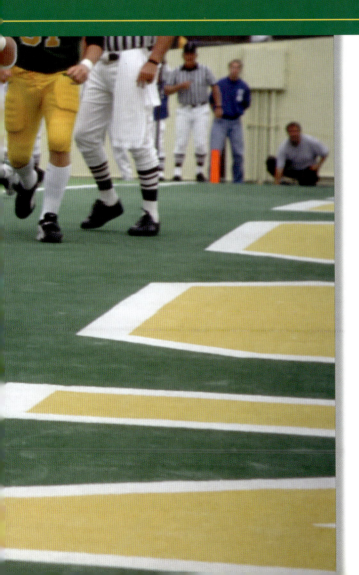

The Greatest Players

Oregon's roster of greats includes many of the Pac-10's preeminent football legends. The names are familiar to fans of college football, and for the fans of the Ducks' rivals, they still bring a shiver of dread.

Oregon has had so many great players that they can't all be included here, which is why the following rundown should be considered representative, not definitive.

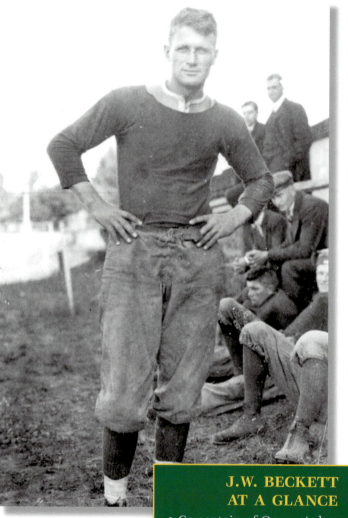

J.W. BECKETT
Halfback/Defensive Tackle
1913–1916

The tackle was captain of Oregon's first Rose Bowl team in 1916 and helped guide the Webfoots to a 14–0 victory against Pennsylvania.

The following season he was captain of the Mare Island Marines that defeated Camp Lewis 19–7 in the Rose Bowl, making him the only player ever to captain two Rose Bowl teams. Both of those teams had undefeated seasons.

Beckett also was a part-time halfback and full-time punter on both. Against Oregon State in 1916, Beckett rushed for 100 yards on 20 carries.

Beckett went on to serve 50 years in the marines, reaching the rank of brigadier general. He coached marine teams at Mare Island in 1920, Quantico from 1921–1924, and San Diego in 1925 and 1931–1932, with a record of 56–19–3. He was assistant coach at Navy from 1926 to 1928.

J.W. BECKETT AT A GLANCE

- Co-captain of Oregon's lone Rose Bowl–winning team (1916)
- Also the co-captain of the Mare Island Marines' undefeated Rose Bowl–winning team of 1917
- Only man to captain two Rose Bowl teams
- Described as a "man who can play any position on a football team"
- An effective punter and running back as well as defensive tackle

JOHN KITZMILLER

Offensive/Defensive Back
1927–1930

The 6'0", 165 pound "Flying Dutchman" gained a reputation for being a great tackler. He was a two-time All–Pacific Coast Conference tailback and defensive back and earned second-team All-America honors as a senior. He scored 14 touchdowns during his career, and Oregon won 23 of 30 games over his three seasons. He also was Oregon's kicker.

Kitzmiller played one season in the NFL with the New York Giants in 1931 before returning to Oregon as an assistant coach for four years. He was inducted into the College Football Hall of Fame in 1969.

JOHN KITZMILLER AT A GLANCE

- Nicknamed the "Flying Dutchman" for his spectacular tackles despite his slight build
- Two-time All Pacific Coast Conference offensive and defensive back
- Scored 14 touchdowns and converted 13 extra points during his career

MEL RENFRO

Running Back/Defensive Back
1961–1963

The speedy two-sport star from Portland turned an All-America college career at Oregon into a Hall-of-Fame professional career with the Dallas Cowboys.

As a running back for the Ducks, Renfro ended his three-year campaign with what was then a school record of 1,540 rushing yards and 141 total points scored.

His best season came in 1962, when the junior rushed for a school-record 753 yards and 10 touchdowns, completed five passes for 114 yards and two touchdowns and caught 16 passes for 298 yards.

In those one-platoon days, Renfro was one of the top defensive backs in the country. He also excelled at track, finishing second in the 1962 NCAA 120-yard high hurdles and helping the Oregon 4x440 team set the world record in 1961.

The Cowboys drafted Renfro as a cornerback in the second round of the 1964 NFL draft. In his 14 seasons in Dallas, Renfro played in 10 straight Pro Bowls, was named All-Pro five times and played in four Super Bowls.

Renfro retired in 1977 but remains the Cowboys' all-time leader in kickoff returns, with a 26.4 average, and interceptions with 52.

He was inducted into the College Football Hall of Fame in 1986. Ten years later, he was enshrined in Canton.

MEL RENFRO AT A GLANCE

- Rushed for 1,540 yards and scored 141 points during his spectacular Oregon career
- Two-sport star finished second in 1962 NCAA 120-yard high hurdles
- Left Oregon with four football and two track records
- Made Pro Bowl appearances in his first 10 seasons with the Cowboys, being named All-Pro five times and playing in four Super Bowls

NORM VAN BROCKLIN

Quarterback

1947–1948

"The Dutchman" was the first in a long line of great Oregon quarterbacks, twice leading the Pacific Coast Conference in passing and once in punting.

In 1948 he led the Ducks to a conference co-championship and their first bowl game in 29 years when Oregon faced off against Southern Methodist on New Year's Day in the 1949 Cotton Bowl.

Van Brocklin's passing numbers were almost twice those of his Cotton Bowl counterpart, the legendary Doak Walker, as he threw for 145 yards and one touchdown to Walker's 79 yards, but the Ducks still lost 21–13.

In all, Van Brocklin led Oregon to 16 wins in 21 games, finished his career with 1,949 passing yards and was named All-American in 1948. He left school with one season of eligibility remaining.

He went on to be a fourth-round draft pick of the Los Angeles Rams in 1949 and spent a 12-year career there and in Philadelphia, amassing 23,611 passing yards and 173 touchdowns. He also averaged 42.9 yards punting.

Van Brocklin led the NFL in passing three times and punting twice while also guiding both the Rams (1951) and Eagles (1960) to NFL championships.

His greatest day as a pro passer came in 1951 when he threw for 554 yards against the New York Yanks, which still stands as an NFL record. That same season he threw a 73-yard pass to Tom Fears to give the Rams a 24–17 victory over the Cleveland Browns in the championship game.

The nine-time Pro Bowler and 1960 league MVP was elected to the College Football Hall of Fame in 1966 and the Pro Football Hall of Fame in 1971.

Van Brocklin was Oregon's first great quarterback, but by no means was he the last. Next, we look at the position where Oregon has had the greatest impact on college football, and it just happens to be football's marquee position.

NORM VAN BROCKLIN AT A GLANCE

- Originator of Oregon's great quarterback legacy
- Led the Pacific Coast Conference twice in passing yards and once in punting
- In 1948, threw for 1,010 yards and led Oregon to a 9–2 record and berth in the Cotton Bowl
- Led both the Rams and the Eagles to NFL Championships
- Named NFL MVP in his final year as a pro, 1960

GEORGE SHAW

1951–1954

One of the greatest and most versatile athletes ever to play at Oregon, Shaw earned All-America honors in both football and baseball and was the No. 1 draft pick by the NFL's Baltimore Colts in 1955.

Shaw began his career at Oregon as a standout defensive back. His 13 interceptions as a freshman in 1951 still stand as a single-season record, and his 18 career picks are the most in school history.

As a sophomore, he set two Pacific Coast Conference passing records when he completed 23 passes on 50 attempts in a 41–7 loss to California.

As a junior, Shaw led the team in passing and also was effective as a wide receiver, with touchdown grabs against San Jose State and one in a 13–7 upset of the USC Trojans.

But Shaw had a breakout season as a senior in 1954. He led the nation in total offense (1,536) and set single-season school records for passing yards (1,358) and total offense.

The Ducks finished 6–4 that year, giving head coach Len Casanova his first winning season.

In his four years as a Duck, Shaw played quarterback, flanker, halfback and defensive back. He was also the punt returner, the punter and kicker. He ended his college career with 3,088 passing yards and 17 touchdowns. He also ran for 420 yards and nine more scores.

His professional career, spent as a quarterback, lasted seven seasons, which he spent with Baltimore, the New York Giants, Minnesota Vikings and Denver Broncos. He threw for 5,829 yards and 41 touchdowns.

GEORGE SHAW AT A GLANCE

- Two-sport All-American (football and baseball)
- Set Oregon's single-season passing record (1,358 yards) and Pacific Coast Conference total offense record (1,536) in 1954
- Led the nation in interceptions (13) in 1951
- Owns school single-season and career interceptions record (18)
- No. 1 pick in the 1955 NFL Draft by Baltimore
- Passed for 5,829 yards and 41 TDs in seven-year pro career

BOB BERRY

1962–1964

Berry was the man under center during the Ducks' most successful three-season stretch in over a quarter-century, and he went on to play in three Super Bowls during a Pro Bowl career in the NFL.

From 1962 to 1964, Berry guided Oregon to three straight winning seasons for the first time since the Ducks had eight straight from 1928 to 1935.

As a junior, he helped Oregon get to the 1963 Sun Bowl, where the Ducks defeated Southern Methodist University 21–14. Playing without two-time All-America running back Mel Renfro, who was out with a wrist injury, Berry led the charge against the Mustangs. He threw touchdown passes of 23 and 20 yards in the second quarter to help the Ducks hold a 21–0 lead at halftime, then settled in as the defense took over in the second half to seal the win. It was Oregon's last bowl game until 1989.

Berry finished his career with 4,297 yards passing and 4,543 yards of total offense. Both

were school bests at the time and still rank among Oregon's top-10 all-time. He also threw for 39 touchdowns and was the first Oregon player to have back-to-back seasons throwing for 1,000 yards or more.

The Ducks were 21–8–2 in his three seasons, with five of those losses coming by a touchdown or less.

Berry would eventually be drafted in the 11th round of the 1964 NFL draft by the Philadelphia Eagles. He played three seasons in Minnesota, then went to Atlanta for five seasons and was a Pro Bowler in 1969 before returning to Minnesota where he was a Viking backup in Super Bowls VIII, IX and XI.

In his 12-year pro career, Berry threw for 9,197 yards and 64 touchdowns.

BOB BERRY
AT A GLANCE

- Guided Ducks to three straight wins for first time in more than 25 years and their first bowl win in 46 seasons
- First Duck to post back-to-back 1,000-yard passing seasons
- Amassed 4,543 yards of total offense and 4,297 yards and 39 TDs passing in his Oregon career
- First-team All-American in 1964
- 12-year NFL career included 9,197 yards passing and 64 touchdowns

DAN FOUTS
1970–1972

Fouts burst onto the scene as a sophomore in 1970, when he took over the quarterback role for an injured Tom Blanchard in the season-opener. He then proceeded to set six single-season school records, tie another and move into third place on the school's all-time passing list—in that one season alone.

By the time the 6'3", 180-pounder out of St. Ignatius High School in San Francisco left Oregon, he had set 19 school records, including total offense (5,871), passing yards (5,995) and touchdown passes (37).

His best statistical season, however, was his first, when as a sophomore he became the first player in school history to surpass the 2,000-yard mark by throwing for 2,390 yards—a record that would stand for 16 years—and set a single-season record with 16 scoring passes.

Though he never played in a bowl game, Fouts engineered the game-winning drive in the Ducks' monumental upset of UCLA in Los Angeles in 1970. Oregon rallied from a 19-point deficit in the final 4:28 in that game to win 41–40. The final score came on a 15-yard touchdown pass from Fouts to end Greg Specht.

Fouts was drafted in the third round by the San Diego Chargers in 1973 and became one of the best and most prolific passers in NFL history. He ended his 14-year professional career with 43,040 passing yards and 254 touchdowns. At the time, he had also established NFL records for 300-yard passing games (51), 3,000-yard seasons (six) and was only the third quarterback to throw for 40,000 yards.

The 1982 NFL MVP and six-time Pro-Bowler also owned 42 team records by the time he retired in 1987. He was inducted into the NFL Hall of Fame in 1993.

DAN FOUTS AT A GLANCE

- Oregon's 1972 MVP
- In 1970, he became the first Oregon quarterback to surpass 2,000 yards passing
- Set school records in total offense (5,871), passing yards (5,995) and touchdown passes (37)
- Enjoyed a stellar, record-setting pro career with the San Diego Chargers, passing for 43,040 career yards and 254 touchdowns
- Named NFL MVP in 1982
- Inducted into the Pro Football Hall of Fame in 1993

CHRIS MILLER
1983–1986

This strong-armed Eugene native did all he could to bust Oregon out of its decade-long slump, setting numerous records as the Ducks transitioned out of a run-oriented offense.

Miller's career as a starter began in 1983, midway through his freshman season, when he took over for the injured Mike Jorgensen. He led the Ducks to a 16–7 upset against Stanford and ended the season in the infamous "Toilet Bowl" Civil War game against Oregon State that was played in below-zero temperatures and ended in a 0–0 tie.

In 1984, Miller came off the bench in the season-opener to guide the Ducks to a 28–17 comeback win against Long Beach State. From there the job was his.

After the Ducks had scored 20 points or more in only five games the previous three seasons, Miller helped Oregon score at least that many in the first three games of 1984. He finished that season throwing for 1,712 yards, the third-best single-season mark in Oregon history.

In 1985, Miller led the conference with 2,237 yards passing and set a school record with 18 touchdown passes. But the Ducks were also last in the Pac-10 in defense and gave up an astounding 204.5 yards per game on the ground.

Miller's senior season was one of the best ever for an Oregon quarterback, as he finally broke Dan Fouts's single-season record for passing yards (2,503) and total offense (2,549), and became the first Pac-10 quarterback to receive first-team all-league honors in consecutive seasons (1985, 1986) in 16 seasons.

He finished his career with 13 overall records. Among those were the records for passing yards (6,681) and total yards of offense (6,841). Both are still fifth all-time at Oregon.

Miller then took his talents to the NFL as the Atlanta Falcons made him the 13th overall selection in the 1987 draft.

In 1991 he led the Falcons to the playoffs and was selected to the Pro Bowl after throwing for 3,103 yards and 26 touchdowns. He concluded his 10-year pro career—which included a three-year hiatus—in 1999 with Denver, having thrown for 19,320 yards and 132 touchdowns.

CHRIS MILLER AT A GLANCE

- The first Pac-10 quarterback to earn consecutive first-team all-league honors in 16 years
- Departed Oregon with 13 school records
- Passed for 6,681 career yards and 42 touchdowns as a collegian
- Completed 60.7 percent of his passes at Oregon
- A Pro Bowl selection for the Atlanta Falcons in 1991

AKILI SMITH

1997–1998

It was a short yet record-setting career for this athletic junior college transfer, who used his strong and accurate arm to produce the most statistically productive season ever for an Oregon quarterback.

Smith transferred to Oregon prior to the 1997 season from Grossmont Junior College in San Diego, where he was a first-team All-American in 1996 following a three-year stint in the Pittsburgh Pirates minor league baseball system.

He started only seven games his first season with the Ducks, but he still managed to pass for 1,385 yards and 13 touchdowns. His 69-yard touchdown pass to Pat Johnson 18 seconds into the 1997 Las Vegas Bowl sparked a 41–13 rout of Air Force.

The following season, under the tutelage of new offensive coordinator Jeff Tedford, Smith produced a season that would vault him into the national spotlight and eventually turn him into the third overall pick in the NFL draft.

The 1998 season opened with No. 23 Michigan State at Autzen Stadium. Behind Smith's 292 total yards and four first-half touchdown passes, the Ducks jumped out to a stunning 34–0 halftime lead. They went on to win 48–14.

In the final four games of the season, Smith threw for 442 yards and three touchdowns in a 27–22 win against Washington, 397 yards and four touchdowns in a 51–19 win against Arizona State, 430 yards and four touchdowns in a 44–41 double-overtime loss in the Civil War to Oregon State, and then 456 yards and two touchdowns in a 51–43 loss to Colorado in the Aloha Bowl.

He ended the season with 3,763 yards passing, 32 touchdowns and 3,947 yards of total offense. All three marks are still the best in school history, and his touchdown passes are the third-best single-season total in the history of the Pac-10.

Only two other Oregon quarterbacks have surpassed 3,000 yards passing, while no player is within 856 yards of his total offense record. He also ended his career with four of the school's top eight single-game passing marks. He still owns three.

Smith's career totals were 5,148 yards passing, 45 touchdowns to only 15 interceptions and 5,515 yards of total offense.

The 1998 Pac-10 Offensive Player of the Year went on to be selected by the Cincinnati Bengals. His disappointing pro career lasted only four seasons.

JOEY HARRINGTON
1998–2001

Joey Harrington wasn't the fastest quarterback in Oregon history, nor did he have the strongest arm. And you won't find Harrington's name sitting at the top of any of the school's numerous all-time quarterback records.

Except for one, that is: winning percentage.

Harrington was great at many things, but he was exceptional at winning. The Portland native and second-generation Oregon quarterback was 25–3 as a starter from 1999 to 2001 and went undefeated in three bowl game appearances, with victories against Minnesota in the 1999 Sun Bowl, Texas in the 2000 Holiday Bowl and Colorado in the 2001 Fiesta Bowl.

The 2001 Heisman Trophy finalist—Oregon's first—finished his career with 512 completions on 928 attempts for 6,911 yards, 59 touchdowns and only 23 interceptions in 33 games. He also added 210 yards and 18 scores on 145 carries.

His 7,121 yards of total offense rank third in school history behind Danny O'Neil (8,124) and Bill Musgrave (8,140), and only O'Neil (8,301) and Musgrave (8,343) have thrown for more yards.

But where Harrington made his biggest mark was in the win column, and that trend began almost immediately.

Harrington had lost an open starting quarterback battle to A.J. Feeley in fall camp prior to his sophomore season of 1999. But when Feeley struggled midway through the season, Harrington stepped in and delivered the goods.

His first significant action came on the road against Arizona in the seventh game of the season, when he replaced Feeley in the third quarter with the Ducks trailing 24–21. Harrington promptly led the Ducks on scoring drives on three of their six possessions as they came from behind to win 44–41.

The following week against Arizona State at Autzen Stadium, Harrington again replaced Feeley to start the second half with the game tied 3–3.

Trailing 17–13 with just over a minute to play, Harrington led the Ducks on a drive that ended with him hitting Marshaun Tucker with a 29-yard touchdown strike with nine seconds left for a 20–17 win.

With that, the "Captain Comeback" era had begun, as Harrington officially became the starter and led the Ducks to victories in their next four games, including the Sun Bowl.

Harrington got Oregon off to a hot start in 2000, guiding the Ducks to consecutive wins against UCLA and Washington, which were both ranked No. 6 at the time.

RB TRANSFERS

In 1996 Oregon plucked former USC recruit Saladin McCullough out of Pasadena City College and brought him to Eugene to jump-start the Ducks' running attack.

Two years later Oregon brought in JC transfer Reuben Droughns, followed by JC transfer Maurice Morris, followed by Tennessee transfer Onterrio Smith.

Those four consecutive transfer starters at running back helped rewrite the Oregon record books. All four are among the school's top-10 all-time total rushing-yard leaders, and combined, they account for six of the Ducks' top-10 single-season rushing totals and six of the top-10 single-game rushing records.

McCullough, a smooth, elusive runner who glided through traffic as if on roller-skates, tied the single-season record with 15 touchdowns as a junior in 1996 while rushing for 685 yards.

One season later, McCullough ran for a school-record 1,343 yards and scored nine touchdowns. He ended the season rushing for 150 yards, including a 76-yard touchdown run, in Oregon's Las Vegas Bowl win against Air Force. He is 10th all-time at Oregon with 2,028 yards.

Droughns followed McCullough and appeared set to break his single-season record when he opened the 1998 season with a 202-yard performance against Michigan State. He went on to rush for 824 yards in only five games before an injury ended his season.

In 1999 Droughns rushed for 1,234 yards—second-most in school history—and finished his career with 2,058 yards and 18 touchdowns. Droughns also owns four of the top-10 single-game rushing totals in Oregon history.

Then came Morris, who in 2000 rushed for 1,188 yards (fifth-best) and eight touchdowns. In 2001 Morris and Smith, who was in his first season, teamed to give the Ducks their first pair of 1,000-yard rushers. Smith led with 1,058 while Morris added 1,049.

Morris finished his career in sixth place all-time at Oregon with 2,237 career yards. Smith went on to add another 1,141 yards in 2002. He also holds the Oregon record for most consecutive 100-yard games, with seven in 2002. He also holds the single-game record, with 285 against Washington State in 2001.

THE TRANSFER LEGACY

PLAYER	YEAR	YARDS	TDS
Saladin McCullough	1997	1,343	9
Reuben Droughns	1999	1,234	9
Maurice Morris	2000	1,188	8
	2001	1,049	9
Onterrio Smith	2001	1,058	7
	2002	1,141	12

Saladin McCullough

Reuben Droughns

Maurice Morris

Onterrio Smith

RB ALPHONSE "TUFFY" LEEMAN

1932

This running back played at Oregon for only one season before moving on to George Washington University, where he gained 2,382 yards on 490 carries in his career.

Leeman was the MVP of the 1936 College Football All-Star Game and became a second-round pick by the New York Giants in the NFL's inaugural draft in 1936.

Leeman led NFL rushers as rookie in 1936 with 830 yards and was named All-NFL in 1936 and 1939. He was second-team All-NFL five times and finished his career with 3,142 yards rushing, 2,324 yards passing, 442 yards receiving and 42 total touchdowns.

He was inducted into the Pro Football Hall of Fame in 1978.

RB AHMAD RASHAD (BOBBY MOORE)

1969–1971

Oregon had never had an offensive threat quite like Bobby Moore and hasn't had one since.

The dazzling talent from Tacoma, Washington, became Oregon's first 1,000-yard rusher and left the school after the 1971 season having established 14 school records, including single-game, season and career rushing records.

He was also the only player ever to lead the conference in scoring from two different positions.

As a sophomore in 1969, Moore rushed for 171 yards on only 22 carries but set an Oregon record with a Pac-8–best 54 catches for 754 yards. His 10 receiving touchdowns and 15 overall scores also led the conference and set new school marks.

Then in 1970 Moore took over the rushing responsibilities and broke Mel Renfro's single-season record with 924 yards and 11 touchdowns—again a league-best.

And as a senior in 1971, Moore became the first Oregon running back to break 1,000 yards when he led the conference with 1,211 rushing yards.

That season Moore earned All-America honors from different publications and was first-team all-conference for the third-straight season.

He was selected with the fourth pick overall by the St. Louis Cardinals in the 1972 NFL draft and later played in a Super Bowl with the Minnesota Vikings and earned four trips to the Pro Bowl.

He is fifth all-time at Oregon, with 2,306 yards rushing and is third all-time in scoring, with 226 points. His 249 yards against Utah in 1971 remain the school's second-best single-game effort.

AHMAD RASHAD (BOBBY MOORE)

YEARS	CARRIES	YARDS	AVG
1969–1971	474	2,306	4.0

RB DEREK LOVILLE

1986–1989

Statistically speaking, there has never been a more productive back at Oregon. The four-year starter is the Ducks' career record-holder with 3,296 yards—making him the only Oregon player with more than 3,000 yards—to go with 45 touchdowns and 5,223 all-purpose yards.

Loville was the first player to lead Oregon in rushing for four straight seasons and one of only four to surpass 1,200 yards in a season. He also had 11 career 100-yard games.

His junior season in 1988 was his best, as he totaled 1,202 yards (fourth-best single-season mark) and 13 rushing touchdowns.

But it was in his senior season that he helped Oregon end a 26-year absence from the postseason, when he rushed for 959 yards in the Ducks' 1989 Independence Bowl campaign.

Loville went on to have a 10-year professional career.

DEREK LOVILLE

YEARS	CARRIES	YARDS	AVG
1986–1989	811	3,296	4.0

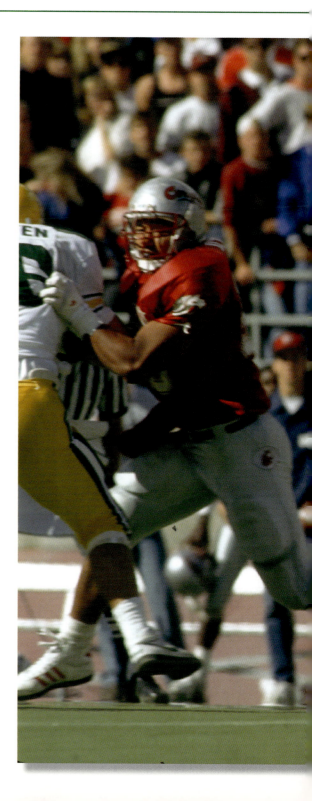

Derek Loville

WR BOB NEWLAND
1968–1970

The Eugene native completed his Oregon career in 1970 as the school leader with 125 receptions for 1,941 yards and 13 touchdowns.

He was the last Duck to lead the conference in receiving when he registered 67 catches and 1,123 yards as a senior, including a 10-catch, 225-yard game against Illinois.

He is still seventh all-time in catches and eighth all-time in yards, while he still owns the top single-season yards mark with his 1970 total.

His 67 catches as a senior remained the single-season record until Samie Parker broke it with 77 grabs in 2003.

Newland was picked in the seventh round by the New Orleans Saints in the 1971 NFL draft. He played for five seasons.

BOB NEWLAND

YEARS	CATCHES	YARDS	AVG
1968–1970	125	1,941	13.5

DL DAVE WILCOX

1962–1963

Oregon's most recent Pro Football Hall of Fame inductee transferred to Oregon from Boise Junior College in 1962 and made his mark as a defensive lineman on teams more remembered for their offensive prowess behind star quarterback Bob Berry and running back Mel Renfro.

Wilcox was a key player in the Ducks' 21–14 victory against Southern Methodist in the 1963 Sun Bowl. Led by Wilcox, the Oregon defense kept the Mustangs off the scoreboard through the first three quarters.

After earning third-team all-Coast honors and being named Oregon's most improved player as a senior, Wilcox went on to be the MVP of the Hula Bowl and later was drafted in the third round by the San Francisco 49ers.

During his 11-year pro career as a linebacker, the Ontario, Oregon, native played in seven Pro Bowls, was named All-NFL five times and earned the nickname "the Intimidator."

He was also know for his durability, missing only one game during his career due to injury.

Wilcox also had two sons who played for Oregon. His eldest son, Josh (1993–1996), was a standout tight end for four seasons and a key performer on the Ducks' 1994 Rose Bowl team as a sophomore. His son Justin (1996–1999) started as a quarterback but then moved to the secondary, where he was a two-year starter. Justin Wilcox is currently the defensive coordinator at Boise State.

Wilcox was elected into the NFL Hall of Fame in 2000.

LB TOM GRAHAM
1969–1971

Linebacker Tom Graham is the most prolific tackler in Oregon history with 433
career stops in three seasons.

That included his outstanding sophomore season in 1969 when he registered
206 total tackles, including 105 unassisted.

For perspective, the Pac-10 Conference
didn't keep official tackling records until
1984, with the current record-holder being
Arizona's Byron Evans with 196. That is
also an NCAA single-season record.

Graham earned his only all-league
honors in 1970 when he was named to the
Pac-8's first team.

DB MARIO CLARK
1972–1975

The first true freshman to start in the defensive backfield for Oregon went on to amass 13
interceptions for the Ducks during his four-
year starting career, including a team-high
three in 1974.

Clark was a pivotal member of the 1974
defense that was ranked second in the Pac-10
and allowed only 10.7 points per game—the
fewest since 1964.

Clark went on to become the Pac-8's first
true freshman to earn Defensive Player of the
Week honors. He was a first-team all-league
member his senior season and was named
defensive MVP of the Senior Bowl.

He went on to be the 18th player chosen in
the 1976 NFL draft by the Buffalo Bills, for
whom he started for eight seasons and was
named to the all-rookie team. He ended his
professional career with 26 total interceptions
and a Super Bowl championship with the 1985
San Francisco 49ers.

DT VINCE GOLDSMITH
1977–1980

At 5'11" and 230 pounds, Vince Goldsmith was an undersized defensive lineman. But that didn't prevent him from having an outstanding career.

The two-time All-Conference first-teamer was the Ducks' first defensive lineman to win the Morris Trophy, given annually to the league's best lineman. As a senior in 1980, he was also named second-team All-American by The Associated Press.

His career began with a 13-tackle performance against Georgia as a true freshman starter. His best statistical season came as a sophomore when he compiled 87 tackles —62 of which were unassisted. He ended his career with 281 tackles, including 34 for lost yardage.

Goldsmith was also the No. 1-ranked high school shot putter as a prep senior in 1977. He went on to star in that event for Oregon, as well, qualifying for the NCAA championships. He remains sixth on the Ducks' all-time list with a heave of 63'10¼".

He went on to play 10 seasons in the Canadian Football League. He was named the CFL's most outstanding rookie in 1981.

LB JOE FARWELL

1989–1992

Linebacker Joe Farwell is the only player in program history to lead the Ducks in tackles for three straight seasons.

From his sophomore season of 1990 to his senior season in 1992, Farwell registered 322 tackles. He finished his career with 393, falling only seven tackles short of becoming Oregon's third player to reach 400 career tackles.

He recorded a career-best 112 tackles as a sophomore and averaged 10 tackles per game as both a junior and senior.

The defenses he anchored twice allowed only 18 points per game. He played in three bowl games and recorded a game-high 15 tackles—12 unassisted—in Oregon's 32–31 loss to Colorado State in the 1990 Freedom Bowl.

LB PETER SIRMON

1996–1999

Only an injury that robbed Peter Sirmon of his junior season kept the talented inside linebacker from being one of Oregon's top-10 all-time tacklers.

As it is, Sirmon's four-year career ended in 1999 with 317 tackles, eight sacks and 32 tackles for a loss of yards—eighth-best all-time.

Sirmon led the Ducks in tackling as both a sophomore and a senior, collecting 115 in 1997 and 109 in 1999. He was named first-team All–Pac-10 both of those seasons.

Sirmon played in every game as a freshman, including starts at inside linebacker against Nevada and Arizona State. He finished his first season second on the team with 69 tackles, including a 17-tackle performance against Fresno State in his first college game.

As a sophomore, he also added 4.5 sacks and 17 tackles for a loss. He earned Pac-10 Player of the Week honors on two occasions that year. The first came after he opened the season with 15 tackles, two sacks and a fumble recovery against Arizona. He also made 11 tackles against UCLA, 12 tackles in the win over Utah and 15 tackles in an upset against No. 6 Washington, in which he recovered a fumble.

In the third game of his junior season, Sirmon suffered a torn pectoral muscle against San Jose State, causing him to miss the final eight games. He finished with 24 tackles and one sack in three games.

Then as a senior, he registered 10 or more tackles against Oregon State (10), Washington (12) and UCLA (18) and ended his career with 16 tackles and a school-record seven tackles for loss in the Sun Bowl victory against Minnesota.

He was drafted by the Tennessee Titans in the fourth round of the 2000 NFL draft.

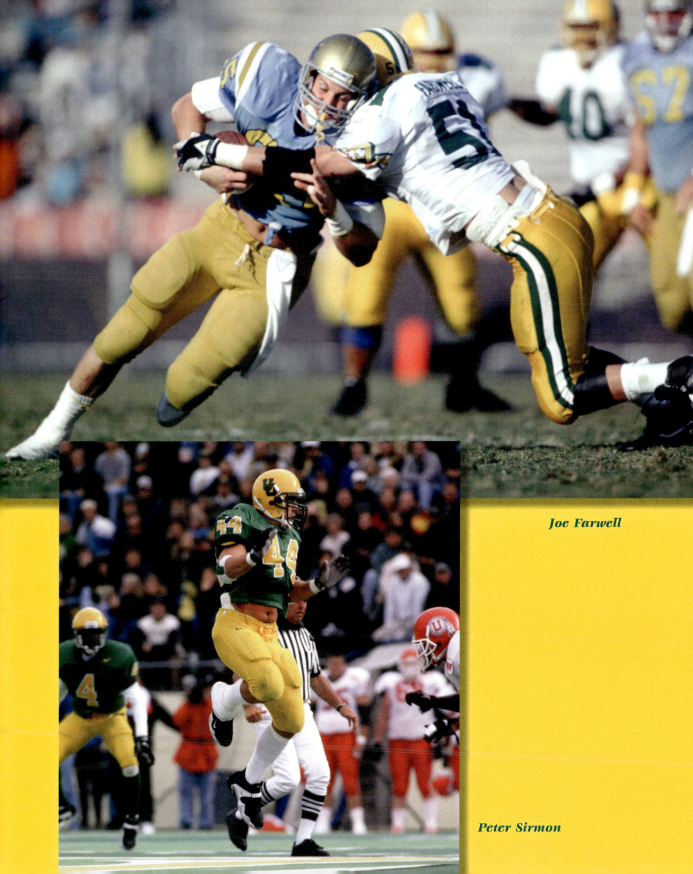

Joe Farwell

Peter Sirmon

DT HALOTI NGATA
2002–2005

This massive defensive lineman came to Oregon in 2002 as the most heralded prep recruit in school history.

Ngata, who boasted a freakish blend of size and speed, was ranked as the top defensive player in the country by *SuperPrep* magazine and PrepStar after recording more than 100 tackles and 30 quarterback sacks as a senior at Highland High School in Salt Lake City, Utah.

He lived up to all expectations, finishing his career at Oregon with 151 tackles (83 solo), 24.5 tackles behind the line of scrimmage, 10 sacks and seven pass deflections in 36 career games (29 starts) before departing for the NFL after his redshirt junior season in 2005. He was the 12th overall pick in the 2006 draft by the Baltimore Ravens.

Ngata also holds the school record with seven blocked kicks.

After missing the season-opener as a freshman in 2002, Ngata played in the final 12 games and was a starter at defensive tackle by the fifth game. He went on to record 44 tackles and 3.5 sacks and finished with a season-high seven tackles against rival Oregon State. The freshmen All-America first-team selection also was named honorable mention All–Pac-10 and earned the Len Casanova Award as the team's top newcomer.

Ngata suffered a season-ending knee injury in the 2003 season-opener against Mississippi State, and though he didn't regain full strength in that knee until midway through his redshirt sophomore season in 2004, he finished the year with a flurry to earn second-team All–Pac-10 honors.

He saw action in 11 games that season, starting nine. He finished fifth on the team with 46 tackles (31 solo), 3.5 sacks and 8.5 tackles for a loss of yards.

Ngata entered his junior season at 6'5", 335 pounds and on a mission. He finished with 61 tackles (32 solo), three sacks, nine tackles for a loss and five pass deflections to win the Pac-10 co-Defensive Player of the Year and the Morris Trophy, given to the Pac-10's top defensive lineman.

He also became Oregon's first consensus All-America first-team selection since defensive back Mel Renfro in 1962.

He went on to earn consensus All-America honors from the NFL Draft Report, Football Writers Association of America, Walter Camp Football Foundation, Sports Illustrated and ESPN.com. Ngata was also a unanimous All–Pac-10 Conference first-team selection and was a finalist for the Outland Trophy (nation's best interior lineman) and the Bronko Nagurski award (best college defensive player).

The following article appeared in the 2005 edition of *Athlon Sports Pac-10 Football Preview*:

BACK WITH A VENGEANCE

Healthy in mind, body and spirit, Haloti Ngata is ready to once again prove himself one of the best defensive linemen in the country. Ngata, a 6'5", 338-pound junior at Oregon, bore that label coming out of Highland High School in Salt Lake City three years ago. The No. 1 defensive line prospect in the nation in 2002, Ngata was perhaps the highest-profile signee ever for the Ducks, and he lived up to his potential by being named a freshman All-American that fall.

But when his father died in a traffic accident just before Oregon's bowl game that year, Ngata's world was shattered. A devout Mormon, he began to question his faith. His grades suffered. Then, in the first quarter of the first game of his sophomore season, the unthinkable happened: he suffered a season-ending knee injury.

The soft-spoken giant who had been on a fast track to the NFL was suddenly broken down.

It has taken two seasons, but this fall, Ngata is again speeding toward the professional ranks. After a dominant second half to the 2004 season, Ngata put off entering the NFL for what is likely just one more year. The explosive tackle is in the best shape of his career, his faith is restored and he is on track for a degree. "If everything works out, I'll plan on entering the draft," says Ngata, a second-team All–Pac-10 selection last season as a sophomore. "I want to be a first-round pick, in the top 25."

Steve Greatwood, Ngata's former position coach who switched to the offensive line at Oregon this season, thinks Ngata can set his goals even higher. "First of all, he's the most intelligent athlete I've ever coached," says Greatwood. "He knows exactly where he needs to be and how it all fits together. So his intelligence allows him to go full-speed, without any hesitation.

"For someone his size, he's got outstanding balance. You can't knock the guy off his feet. And then there's his explosion, getting his mass going forward. There's some technical things he needs to work on, but if he does that, there's no doubt in my mind he'll be a top-10 draft pick."

Those were the lofty expectations that followed Ngata to Oregon when he picked the Ducks over Brigham Young. As a freshman, Ngata started the final eight games of the regular season. Relying on that blend of remarkable quickness and sheer strength, Ngata posted 3.5 sacks and showed a knack for blocking kicks, doing so three times. Ngata was a bright spot in an otherwise dreary season.

The Ducks were preparing for the now-defunct Seattle Bowl when Ngata got word from home—his father, Solomone, had died in a traffic accident less than three weeks before the game.

Ngata's thoughts immediately turned to his mother. He should return home to support her, he thought. Olga Ngata, however, would have none of that. "She wanted me to stay in school, and I know my dad wanted me to finish," Haloti Ngata says. "I wanted to do it for him, make him proud."

Ngata played in the Seattle Bowl, yet another loss for the Ducks.

Oregon head coach Mike Bellotti has since admitted that the team was uninspired during the ensuing offseason, but that was particularly so for Ngata. He stopped attending church functions, and started to gain weight. His thoughts drifted back to his mother.

"The offseason between his freshman and sophomore year, he was questioning a lot of things," Greatwood says. "Not only his weight, but if this was where he needed to be—did he need to be at home with his mother? Because of his ability, it wasn't outwardly apparent that his football waned, but he wasn't playing up to his true ability."

A back injury further limited Ngata in fall camp of 2003. Still, he had enough sheer talent to make the starting lineup for the season opener at Mississippi State. But in the first quarter, Ngata hurt two ligaments in his left leg, ending his season. For Oregon, it was a crushing blow to the defense. To Ngata, it was a wakeup call.

"I had drifted away from being religious," he says. "Thinking that I was unstoppable—not cocky, but thinking I didn't need God. I feel like I got injured for a reason. It humbled me."

The following year was arduous. Ngata had surgery three weeks after the injury and was granted a medical hardship for the year, saving himself a season of eligibility. His body mass made the rehabilitation process slow, and his grades again slipped.

The following spring, however, Greatwood saw signs that Ngata was getting his life—and skills—back on track. "Here's a kid that had never been hurt before," Greatwood says. "They all have that aura of invincibility, and particularly him. Then all of a sudden he's flat on his back. Once he started overcoming that self-doubt, he rededicated himself."

Ngata eased into the 2004 season as he continued to work himself into shape. Through five games, he had only 18 tackles. But in the third quarter of Oregon's sixth game, at home against Arizona, Ngata came to life. He recorded one sack and hurried the quarterback into throwing an incompletion. He stuffed a receiver on a screen play and stopped running backs for lost yardage three different times.

In that single quarter, Ngata posted five tackles, three for negative yards. "That was the game I felt like I was really comfortable being back on the field and injury-free," he says. "I felt more dominant, back to myself."

Halftime of the Arizona game was the exact midway point of Oregon's season. Up to that point, Ngata had 20 tackles, 1.5 for a loss, and no sacks. He finished the year with 46 tackles, 8.5 for a loss, with 3.5 sacks.

"I don't believe Haloti has played his best football for an entire season yet," Greatwood says. "The last five games of last season is a glimpse of what he can be."

"I've coached a lot of good defensive linemen who are in the NFL, and he's right up there," defensive line coach Michael Gray says. "He's got the physical tools. Now it's a matter of him playing enough, and at a high level."

His faith renewed and his body intact, Ngata is primed to do just that for Oregon this fall.

Chad Cota was a tackling machine from his safety spot.

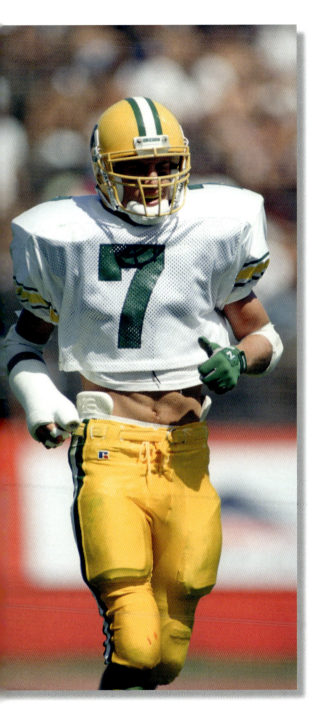

SS CHAD COTA
1991–1994

Playing in a secondary that would produce four NFL draft picks, strong safety Chad Cota was the glue that held it all together.

The former Class 3A state defensive player of the year out of Ashland, Oregon, Cota anchored the famed Gang Green defense in the Ducks' 1994 Rose Bowl season.

As a senior in 1994, the team defensive MVP and first-team All-American finished with 98 tackles and two interceptions and played a pivotal role in numerous victories on the Ducks' path to their Pac-10 championship.

Cota had 12 tackles in the season-turning 31–20 win against Washington and followed that with 11 tackles, an interception and three pass deflections in a 10–9 upset of eighth-ranked Arizona a week later.

Along with starting cornerbacks Herman O'Berry and Alex Molden, free safety Jeff Sherman and sensational newcomer Kenny Wheaton, Cota was part of a defensive backfield ranked as the seventh-best in the nation in the preseason.

That group went on to help the Ducks' defense rank 26th overall in 1994.

Cota and O'Berry would go on to be seventh-round 1995 NFL draft choices. Cota was picked by Carolina, O'Berry by St. Louis. Molden lasted one more season before leaving school after his junior year. Molden, the school record-holder for pass breakups with 60, was the 11th overall pick by the New Orleans Saints in 1996.

Cota started 43 straight games in his Oregon career and finished with 336 tackles (tied for seventh-most in school history) and eight interceptions.

As a freshman, Cota finished with 83 tackles. He then led the team as a junior with 86 tackles and intercepted passes in four straight games.

CB KENNY WHEATON
1994–1996

No player in the history of Oregon football has ever been as defined by one play as Kenny Wheaton has been by "the Pick."

When Wheaton stepped in front of a pass from Washington quarterback Brock Huard and raced 97 yards for the game-clinching touchdown in the final minute against the Huskies in 1994, it became the most memorable moment of the Ducks' unlikely run to their first Rose Bowl in 37 seasons.

That play, still shown before the start of every Oregon home game, stands as the watershed moment for a Ducks football program that, since the 1994 season, has become successful and respected on a national level year in and year out.

Wheaton was a redshirt freshman reserve cornerback in that game against the Huskies, playing in a senior-laden backfield that included future pros Chad Cota, Alex Molden and Herman O'Berry.

He finished his freshman season with 53 tackles and four interceptions. As a sophomore, he had five interceptions, and as a junior he had two, leading the team all three seasons.

Wheaton was also the Ducks' top tackler in 1996, recording 73 to bring his career total to 205. He earned all-league honors all three of his seasons but was a first-team selection only in 1996.

Following the 1996 season, Wheaton became Oregon's first player to leave school early for the NFL draft. He was a 1997 third-round pick by the Dallas Cowboys, playing in 22 games before injuries ended his NFL career. Wheaton then played a season in the Arena League before moving on to the Canadian Football League.

Rich Brooks

The Coaches

It has taken the leadership of great men to produce the legacy and tradition that embody Oregon football.

HUGO BEZDEK
1906, 1913–1917

With the recommendation of a coaching icon, this stocky son of Czech immigrants was hired as Oregon's first full-time football coach in 1906, thus starting what would become a Hall of Fame career.

Bezdek's .727 winning percentage (30–10–4) in his six seasons coaching the Webfoots remains the best in school history for any coach with more than two seasons of service.

His first team went 5–0–1, allowed only 10 points the entire season and implemented the forward pass in its offensive attack. He helped provide players with a training table during the season and required all 35 players to learn every position on the field.

But the 23-year-old Bezdek left the team after only one season to attend medical school at the University of Chicago, where he had once played for and coached under the legendary Amos Alonzo Stagg, whose influence helped Bezdek land the Oregon job.

Bezdek returned to Oregon in 1913 after a stint as football coach and athletic director at Arkansas, where he is credited with giving the school its Razorback nickname.

In 1916, Bezdek's fifth season with the team, Oregon finished 7–0–1 and went to its first Rose Bowl. In that game against the heavily favored University of Pennsylvania Quakers, the Webfoots controlled the ball and kept their opponent off the scoreboard for a 14–0 victory.

Though he returned for one more season, it was apparent Bezdek was looking to leave Oregon when he became manager of Major League Baseball's Pittsburgh Pirates midway through the summer of 1917.

He was back at Oregon in time to coach the Webfoots in the fall of 1917, and though they didn't make a return trip to the Rose Bowl that season, Bezdek did, filling in to coach the Mare Island Marines to a 19–7 win against the Army team from Camp Lewis.

He left Oregon for good after that season to coach football at Penn State, where he was 65–30–11 with two undefeated seasons and one Rose Bowl appearance—making him one of the few men who coached three different teams in the Rose Bowl.

In 1937 Bezdek coached the Cleveland Rams of the National Football League. He remains the only person ever to serve as a head coach in the NFL and a manager in MLB.

Bezdek was inducted into the College Football Hall of Fame in 1954.

HUGO BEZDEK AT A GLANCE	
YEAR	RECORD
1906	5–0–1
1913	3–3–1
1914	4–2–1
1915	7–2
1916	7–0–1
1917	4–3
Total	30–10–4

LEN CASANOVA AT A GLANCE

YEAR	RECORD
1951	2–8
1952	2–7–1
1953	4–5–1
1954	6–4
1955	6–4
1956	4–4–2
1957	7–4
1958	4–6
1959	8–2
1960	7–3–1
1961	4–6
1962	6–3–1
1963	8–3
1964	7–2–1
1965	4–5–1
1966	3–7
Total	82–73–8

LEN CASANOVA

1951–1966

When Len "Cas" Casanova was lured away from the University of Pittsburgh in 1951, Oregon was looking for a savior. It found one in the great gentleman from California, who quickly turned around the Ducks' fortunes and forged a relationship with the school that lasted 52 years.

Cas, who is widely considered the most important figure in the history of Oregon athletics, was the football coach from 1951 to 1966, the athletic director from 1967 to 1970, and after assisting with the completion of Autzen Stadium, stayed active into the new century. He was associated with numerous fund-raising and special projects that improved the Oregon athletic facilities significantly.

"Everything that Oregon athletics is today, it owes to Len Casanova," said recently retired former UO athletic director Bill Moos, following Casanova's passing in 2002.

During his 21-year collegiate coaching career that began at Santa Clara in 1946, Casanova built a 104–97–10 overall record.

At Oregon he went to three bowl games, including the 1958 Rose Bowl, and built an 82–73–8 record, making him the program's winningest head coach until Rich Brooks passed him in 1994. He is now third all-time behind Brooks and Mike Bellotti.

His 1957 team finished the season with a 10–7 loss to Woody Hayes's No. 1–ranked Ohio State team in the 1958 Rose Bowl. The Ducks went into that game as three-touchdown underdogs but refused to accept the odds, keeping it close against the more heralded Buckeyes. Oregon outgained Ohio State in total yards and recorded more first downs. Only a missed 24-yard field goal in the fourth quarter and an unfortunate fumble following Ohio State's go-ahead field goal late in the game stood between the Ducks and a monumental upset.

Casanova's 1958 team ranked second in the country in scoring defense, allowing an average of only five points per game and only surrendering more than seven points once during the entire season.

He coached two NFL Hall of Famers (Mel Renfro and Dave Wilcox) and helped assistants John McKay, John Robinson and George Seifert to their own illustrious coaching careers.

Cas began his 16th and final season at Oregon as the 14th-winningest coach in the country. He was elected to the National Football Foundation Hall of Fame in 1977, and in 1990 he was awarded the Amos Alonzo Stagg Award by the American Football Coaches Association for his outstanding contributions to the sport.

RICH BROOKS

1977–1994

When Rich Brooks left Oregon after 18 seasons, he departed having coached—and won—the most games in school history.

And yet, if it weren't for the Ducks' magical Rose Bowl season of 1994—Brooks's last at the school—who knows how he would have been remembered?

As it stands, Brooks is considered the man who took over at Oregon when the program was as downtrodden as it ever has been and helped to build it into a team that would one day challenge for the national title.

Brooks finished his time at Oregon with a 91–109–4 record and four bowl games under his belt. Remarkably, 39 of those wins and all four postseason appearances came in his final six seasons, with the most notable being his last, when the Ducks finished the regular season 9–3, champions of the Pac-10 and Rose Bowl–bound for the first time in 37 years.

Brooks won the Bear Bryant Award as the National Coach of the Year from the Football Writers Association of America that season, was chosen the Pac-10 Coach of the Year and became the first coach in school history to take the Ducks to four bowl games.

In the Rose Bowl against a powerhouse Penn State team and legendary head coach Joe Paterno, Brooks's troops were locked in a 14–14 tie late in the third quarter before the Nittany Lions pulled away for a 38–20 victory.

Ironically, that 1994 season began with a 1–2 record for the Ducks, and Brooks found himself under siege by fans who wanted him gone.

He did leave after the season, but not because he was fired. Brooks moved on to the NFL, where he coached three seasons with the St. Louis Rams. He is currently back in the college ranks at Kentucky.

Though it took a while for Brooks to get Oregon back into the annual bowl picture, he did have some success early on.

The Ducks' 6–5 record in 1979 was their first winning mark since the 1970 season, and Brooks was named Pac-10 Coach of the Year and the District IX Coach of the Year by the American Football Coaches Association.

Another winning season in 1980 gave Oregon back-to-back winning seasons for the first time in 16 years.

Then in 1989, behind the play of star quarterback Bill Musgrave, the Ducks earned a berth in the Independence Bowl where they defeated Tulsa. It was the Ducks' first bowl berth and eight-win season in 26 years.

Brooks took the team to the 1990 Freedom Bowl—marking the first back-to-back bowl berths in school history—and the 1992 Independence Bowl, although the Ducks lost both games.

The former Oregon State defensive back also had a sterling 14–3–1 record against archrival Oregon State in the annual Civil War game.

Brooks also held the dual role of head coach and athletic director from 1992 to 1994. In recognition of his numerous contributions to the school, Oregon named its football field Brooks Field in his honor in 1995.

**RICH BROOKS
AT A GLANCE**

YEAR	RECORD
1977	2–9
1978	2–9
1979	6–5
1980	6–3–2
1981	2–9
1982	2–8–1
1983	4–6–1
1984	6–5
1985	5–6
1986	5–6
1987	6–5
1988	6–6
1989	8–4
1990	8–4
1991	3–8
1992	6–6
1993	5–6
1994	9–4
Total	91–109–4

MIKE BELLOTTI AT A GLANCE

YEAR	RECORD
1995	9–3
1996	6–5
1997	7–5
1998	8–4
1999	9–3
2000	10–2
2001	11–1
2002	7–6
2003	8–5
2004	5–6
2005	10–2
2006	7–6
Total	97–48

MIKE BELLOTTI
1995–Present

The current Oregon head coach has guided the Ducks to the most prosperous and successful decade of football in school history and has become the program's winningest coach along the way.

Bellotti passed his predecessor Rich Brooks in the second week of the 2006 season with a victory at Fresno State to set the new record of 92 career wins.

The "dean of the Pac-10" is tied for eighth all-time in conference wins (60–37), and only four former Pac-10 coaches (John Robinson, Don James, Terry Donahue and Larry Smith) were able to record more conference wins than Bellotti in their first 10 years in the league.

Bellotti currently sports a 97–48 record at Oregon—and a 111–67–2 record overall—and a winning percentage of 68.2 percent that trails only Hugo Bezdek's 72.7 percent among Oregon head coaches who were with the Ducks a minimum of three seasons.

Bellotti guided Oregon to the No. 2 ranking in the country and a BCS bowl game win in 2001. Overall, he has led the school to 10 bowl appearances in his 12 years. His teams went to seven straight bowl games from 1997 to 2003, an amazing accomplishment for a program that had posted back-to-back bowl game years only twice before in its history.

Bellotti's teams have recorded eight or more wins in a single season seven times and accumulated the second-most victories of any program in the Pac-10 during his tenure. He has overseen a program that has finished among the nation's Top 20 four times in the past eight seasons.

Only six active Division I coaches in the country have guided their current schools to more postseason appearances than Bellotti has at Oregon, and he's the only coach to lead the Ducks to four postseason wins.

The most notable season of Bellotti's remarkable tenure came in 2001, when Bellotti coached the Ducks to their first-ever 11-win season, a campaign that ended with Oregon's crushing of Colorado, 38–16, in the Fiesta Bowl to finish with an all-time high national ranking of second in the Associated Press and USA Today/ESPN Coaches polls.

Bellotti has been influential in the development of four Pacific-10 all-conference quarterbacks—Bill Musgrave in 1990, Danny O'Neil in 1994 (who completed his career as the Rose Bowl co-MVP), Akili Smith in 1998 (Oregon's first Pac-10 Offensive Player of the Year) and Joey Harrington in 2001 (Pac-10 Offensive Player of the Year and a Heisman Trophy finalist).

In addition, his system has produced three sets of two 1,000-yard passers in the same season—a feat that had never been accomplished in school history prior to Bellotti's arrival.

While the faces have changed, Bellotti's system has been responsible for Oregon's ranking among the nation's top 20 teams in passing offense in eight of the last 14 years under 10 different quarterbacks as well as five different coordinators. Oregon led the Pac-10 Conference in scoring his initial year as offensive coordinator in 1989 as well as his first year as head coach.

Mike Bellotti

THE ASSISTANTS

Oregon has also been a training ground for some of history's most successful coaches in both the collegiate and professional ranks.

John McKay, the famed USC coach and inaugural leader of the Tampa Bay Buccaneers, got his start as both a player and coach for Len Casanova. He was a Casanova assistant for eight seasons before leaving in 1959 for the Trojans, who he guided to four national championships (1962, 1967, 1972 and 1974). His 1972 squad is regarded as one of the best teams in NCAA history. Two of his players, Mike Garrett (1965) and O.J. Simpson (1968), won the Heisman Trophy. He popularized the I-formation, emphasizing a power running game.

After turning down several offers from NFL teams, McKay was lured to Tampa Bay to become the Buccaneers' first head coach in 1976.

His replacement at USC was none other than John Robinson, who played under both Cas and McKay at Oregon from 1955 to 1958. He then was a Duck assistant from 1960 to 1971.

Robinson's USC teams won 82 percent of their games (67–14–2) in his original run, averaging nearly 10 victories per year. Robinson tied a NCAA record for most wins by a first-year head coach after his team went 11–1 and earned a Rose Bowl berth in 1976.

He won the 1978 national championship and led the Trojans to three Pac-10 titles before leaving for the Los Angles Rams in 1983. He returned to USC for the 1993–1997 seasons.

Other Duck assistant coaches included George Seifert, who went on to win two Super Bowl titles with the San Francisco 49ers in 1989 and 1994, and Bruce Snyder, who was at Oregon from 1964 to 1971 as a running backs/quarterbacks coach. He became the head coach at Arizona State and won Pac-10 Coach of the Year honors in 1990 and 1996. His 1996 team also won the conference title.

Current head coach Mike Bellotti has also spawned a handful of successful head coaches. Jeff Tedford was offensive coordinator for the Ducks from 1998 to 2001 before taking the head coaching job at California. The man he replaced at Oregon, Dirk Koetter, left the Ducks in 1997 after a two-year stint to become the head coach at Boise State. Koetter eventually left the Broncos for Arizona State. In 2006 Chris Petersen, a wide receivers coach for Oregon from 1995 to 2000, led Boise State to a 13-0 record in his first season as head coach and a historic upset in the Fiesta Bowl against Oklahoma.

Danny O'Neil (No. 16) led the Ducks to the 1995 Rose Bowl.

Duck Superlatives

Oregon football history is littered with moments of greatness—outstanding seasons, great games played, superior individual efforts, memorable upsets and more. Here is a small sample of that record of achievement.

The Great Teams

THE 1994 SEASON

For Oregon football, there is the era before October 22, 1994, and there is everything after. Without question, that was the afternoon when the program's fortunes changed for good.

The momentum gained under quarterback Bill Musgrave through 1990 was beginning to wane entering the season. With Danny O'Neil at quarterback and Rich Brooks assuming the dual role of head coach and athletic director, the Ducks had gone 5–6 in 1993, including a horrific loss to Cal in which they blew a 30–0 halftime lead and then a three-game losing streak to end the year. It was Oregon's third straight season without a winning record.

But in 1994, O'Neil was a senior, with a talented array of weapons in receiver Cristin McLemore, tight end Josh Wilcox and the tailback tandem of Dino Philyaw and Ricky Whittle. On the other side of the ball was the "Gang Green" defense, built around linebackers Jeremy Asher, Rich Ruhl and Reggie Jordan, and a secondary that included Chad Cota, Alex Molden, Herman O'Berry and a talented freshman corner-back named Kenny Wheaton.

The 1994 campaign got off to a sloppy 1–2 start, with losses to Hawaii and Utah. But the Ducks cleaned it up to surprise Iowa in Eugene, then won at USC behind backup quarterback Tony Graziani. O'Neil missed that game with an infection in his hand, then had to come off the bench the following week in a loss at Washington State when Graziani was hurt. Oregon rebounded to beat Cal, and the Ducks were 4–3 with a visit from No. 9 Washington up next.

The Huskies were the bullies of the Northwest, having won nearly two-thirds of the games against Oregon to that point in the series. It appeared that trend would continue when Washington took a 20–17 lead midway through the fourth quarter, until O'Neil mounted the first comeback of his career. He marched the Ducks 98 yards to the touchdown that put them ahead 24–20.

Less than three minutes remained when the Huskies took possession, and they calmly drove down to Oregon's 8-yard line behind running back Napoleon Kaufman and quarterback Damon Huard. What happened next has

been replayed countless times on the video scoreboard at Autzen Stadium. It is known simply as "the Pick."

With 1:08 remaining, Huard dropped back to pass and looked to his left. Receiver Dave Janoski ran an out pattern, but Wheaton timed it perfectly and stepped in front for the interception. He raced up the sideline, split two Huskies near midfield and scampered into the end zone to complete a 97-yard return. Oregon football, in the minds of the program, its fans and opponents, would never be the same.

The next week, the Ducks knocked off another top-10 team, beating No. 8 Arizona. Wins over Arizona State, Stanford and Oregon State followed, with Philyaw scoring on a screen pass late in the fourth quarter to beat the Beavers 17–13. Oregon, so long a conference also-ran, was the Pac-10's champion and Rose Bowl representative.

The No. 9 Ducks met mighty Penn State as the decided underdog in Pasadena. The second-ranked Nittany Lions of Kerry Collins and Ki-Jana Carter were expected to dismantle the Ducks. Instead, O'Neil threw for what was then a game record 456 yards, and Oregon held its own in a 38–20 defeat.

The Ducks had earned the respect of the nation, going 9–4 to tie the school record for wins. That proved to be the final season in Eugene for Brooks, who was named head coach of the St. Louis Rams. Offensive coordinator Mike Bellotti took over and took the team to even bigger heights over the next decade. But it all began that afternoon in October, when Wheaton stepped in front of a pass and the Ducks stepped into the national spotlight.

1994 OREGON DUCKS

September 3	Portland State	W	58–16
September 10	at Hawaii	L	16–36
September 17	Utah	L	16–34
September 24	Iowa	W	40–18
October 1	at USC	W	22–7
October 8	Washington State	L	7–21
October 15	California	W	23–7
October 22	Washington	W	31–20
October 29	Arizona	W	10–9
November 5	Arizona State	W	34–10
November 12	at Stanford	W	55–21
November 19	at Oregon State	W	17–13
January 2	Penn State*	L	20–38

*Rose Bowl

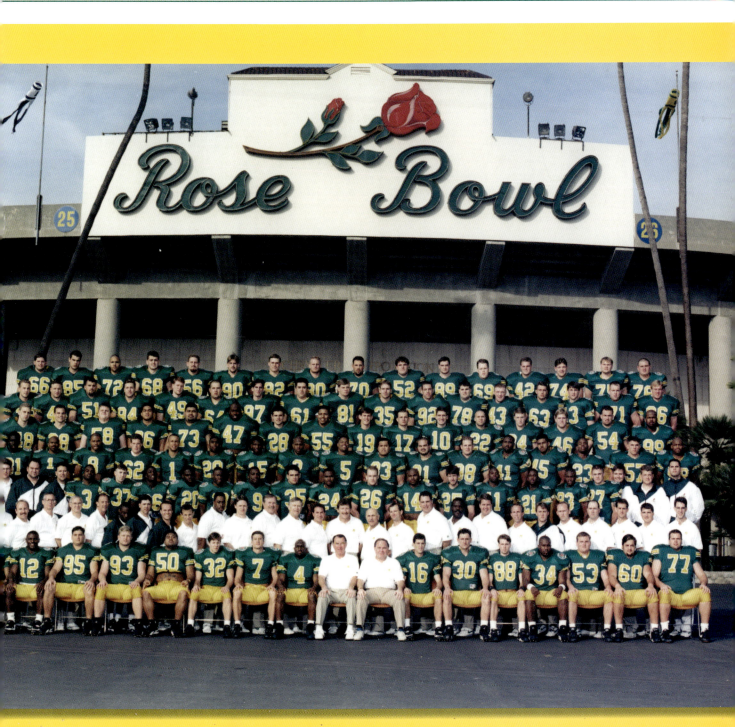

The 1994 Ducks at the Rose Bowl

After opening the 1998 season with 200-yard rushing performances in three of the Ducks' first five games, Reuben Droughns suffered a broken leg versus UCLA, damaging the Ducks' prospects.

1998 OREGON DUCKS

September 5	Michigan State	W	48–14
September 12	at UTEP	W	33–26
September 19	San Jose State	W	58–3
September 26	Stanford	W	63–28
October 10	at Washington State	W	51–29
October 17	at UCLA	L	38–41 ot
October 24	USC	W	17–13
October 31	at Arizona	L	3–38
November 7	Washington	W	27–22
November 14	Arizona State	W	51–19
November 21	at Oregon State	L	41–44 2ot
December 25	Colorado*	L	43–51

*Aloha Bowl

THE 1998 SEASON

For all the success other Oregon teams have had, there are some who will argue—convincingly—that the 1998 version was the most talented team in school history. The offense set school records for points and yards per game, and the defense was a group of tough overachievers personified by inspirational end Saul Patu, spirited safety Michael Fletcher and linebacker Chris Vandiver, who filled in admirably after an injury to Peter Sirmon.

The previous season had been an inconsistent one, as the Ducks dealt with a rotating quarterback system that coach Mike Bellotti would employ often in the future. Akili Smith showed promise as a junior college transfer, but he shared the job with Jason Maas. Oregon went just 6–5 in the regular season, but a Civil War victory gave the Ducks a winning record and a spot in the Las Vegas Bowl, where they trounced Air Force and set the tone for the following season.

In 1998 Smith flourished under the tutelage of offensive coordinator Jeff Tedford. Smith had a dependable set of receivers that included Damon Griffin and Tony Hartley, and a veteran offensive line. In addition, the Ducks signed another JC transfer, running back Reuben Droughns, who provided the toughness that complemented Smith's flash.

Droughns rushed for over 200 yards in three of Oregon's first five games, wins over Michigan State, Stanford and Washington State. The Ducks also beat Texas-El Paso and San Jose State in that early stretch, but Droughns

injured his ankle against the Miners and didn't play against the Spartans. It was a chilling omen of things to come.

The Ducks were 5–0 and ranked No. 11 when they went south to meet No. 2 UCLA. The eyes of the nation were on the game, including ESPN's College Football GameDay crew. Oregon trailed 24–14 at halftime, then scored 17 straight to take a fourth-quarter lead. UCLA was unbowed, answering back with two touchdowns, the second set up by Droughns's third fumble of the day. The Ducks scored to tie the game, then survived a missed field goal as time expired, but Smith threw an interception in overtime, and the Bruins scored to win 41–38.

As big as the loss that day was the one that lingered throughout the season, as Droughns had suffered a broken leg at some point during his 172-yard performance. The Ducks rebounded to beat USC 17–13 thanks in large part to a 62-yard touchdown run by Smith, but they were embarrassed by Trung Canidate and Arizona to fall to 6–2. A dramatic double overtime loss to Oregon State closed the regular season, and Oregon went on to the Aloha Bowl, where the Ducks lost to Colorado.

In the bowl game, Smith passed for 456 yards, Griffin and Hartley each had at least 146 receiving yards and Derien Latimer ran for three touchdowns. That was a microcosm of a season, in which the Ducks averaged nearly 40 points and 483 yards of offense per game and also came up just short despite having so much talent.

Captain Comeback

THE 1999 AND 2000 TEAMS

*Joey Harrington,
Captain Comeback*

1999 OREGON DUCKS

September 2	at Michigan State	L	20–27	
September 11	UTEP	W	47–28	
September 18	Nevada	W	72–10	
September 25	USC	W	33–30	3ot
October 2	at Washington	L	20–34	
October 9	at UCLA	L	29–34	
October 23	at Arizona	W	44–41	
October 30	Arizona State	W	20–17	
November 6	Washington State	W	52–10	
November 13	at California	W	24–19	
November 20	Oregon State	W	25–14	
December 31	Minnesota*	W	24–20	

*Sun Bowl

Not the first quarterback to be dubbed "Captain Comeback," Joey Harrington nevertheless earned the nickname in spades during his tenure at Oregon. His greatest example of snatching victory from the jaws of defeat came in 2000, but not before Harrington gave fans a preview of things to come.

A.J. Feeley began the 1999 season as Oregon's starter and directed the Ducks to a 3–3 start. In week seven of that season, at Arizona, Harrington came off the bench during a back-and-forth game and helped Oregon score the final 10 points late in the fourth quarter of a 44–41 victory. The following week, in Eugene, Harrington replaced Feeley at half-time and again dug the Ducks out of a hole, throwing the game-winning touchdown pass with nine seconds left in a 20–17 win over Arizona State.

That was the last time Harrington came off the bench in an Oregon uniform. He started the final four games of that season, capping it with more dramatics in the Sun Bowl. Harrington accounted for all three touchdowns in the 24–20 victory over Minnesota, running for two scores and throwing the game-winning touchdown pass in the fourth quarter.

Having clinched the starting job, Harrington got the Ducks off to a 6–1 start in 2000, the lone loss coming at Wisconsin. Among the victories was a 29–10 win over UCLA, in which the Ducks scored the final 19 points, followed by wins over Washington and USC.

Thus, the Ducks were ranked seventh in the nation when they traveled to play Arizona

Samie Parker's spectacular catch versus USC was one of the many highlights of the 2000 Ducks' 10-2 season.

State on October 28, 2000. That became the day Harrington permanently assumed the title of "Captain Comeback" within the borders of the Beaver State.

The game was so even, each team scored the same amount of points in each quarter. Harrington threw for 434 yards and a school record–tying six touchdowns, while ASU quarterback Jeff Krohn answered with 432 yards and five touchdowns.

Arizona State scored twice early in the fourth quarter to take a 42–28 lead, then matched an Oregon touchdown to make it 49–35 with 5:47 left. That's when Harrington really went to work, throwing a 32-yard touchdown pass to Marshaun Tucker with 3:21 to play. The Ducks got the ball back and drove deep into Sun Devils territory, but on fourth-and-goal from the 9-yard line, Oregon tight end Justin Peelle was stuffed at the 1-yard line.

Needing only to run out the clock, Arizona State fumbled, with Jermaine Hanspard recovering Mike Williams's gaffe. One play later, Peelle redeemed himself by catching a 17-yard touchdown pass that tied the game with 27 seconds left.

Each team misfired in overtime, Krohn throwing the game's only interception and the Ducks missing a field goal. In the second overtime, Harrington directed a drive that ended with Allan Amundson's one-yard touchdown

2000 OREGON DUCKS			
September 2	Nevada	W	36–7
September 9	at Wisconsin	L	23–27
September 16	Idaho	W	42–13
September 23	UCLA	W	29–10
September 30	Washington	W	23–16
October 14	at USC	W	28–17
October 21	Arizona	W	14–10
October 28	at Arizona State	W	56–55 2ot
November 4	at Washington State	W	27–24 ot
November 11	California	W	25–17
November 18	at Oregon State	L	13–23
December 29	Texas*	W	35–30

*Holiday Bowl

run and the extra point. Arizona State quickly scored on a 22-yard touchdown pass and also set up to kick the extra point. But with an injured kicker and a secondary worn out by chasing Harrington's receivers all day, the Sun Devils faked. Krohn looked to tight end Todd Heap for the two-point conversion, but Heap couldn't secure the pass, and Harrington had secured his legacy.

The Ducks won in overtime again a week later, getting a Harrington-to-Tucker touchdown pass and a two-point conversion to tie the game with Washington State at 24 in the fourth quarter. Josh Frankel then kicked the game-winning field goal in overtime, atoning for his miss the week before, and Oregon's Jed Boice blocked an attempt to tie by Washington State.

The Ducks were ranked No. 5 entering the Civil War against the No. 8 Beavers, their Rose Bowl hopes still alive. But Oregon State scored two quick touchdowns, and Harrington had his worst game in an Oregon uniform, throwing five interceptions and losing a fumble.

The loss dropped the Ducks into the Holiday Bowl, where they met Texas. Harrington ran, caught and passed for touchdowns, and the Ducks scored the tiebreaking touchdown with 5:46 left in the fourth quarter. They later took an intentional safety while running out the clock and held on to beat the Longhorns 35–30. For the next few months Oregon celebrated its first 10-win season, and fans wondered if the 2000 team might have been the school's best ever. Just one year later, those arguments were forgotten, as Harrington carried the team to even greater heights.

THE 2001 SEASON

Beginning in 1996, a trend developed for the Oregon football team that mapped the program's leap from Pac-10 Conference also-ran to national title contender. The Ducks won six games that season, then seven in 1997. They won eight in 1998, then nine, then 10 in 2000. By 2001, Oregon's success was off the charts. The Ducks won an unprecedented 11 games that season, topping it with a resounding defeat of Colorado in the Fiesta Bowl to finish the year ranked second in the nation.

The 2001 team was built using talented skill players and overachieving lines. Quarterback Joey Harrington, having established himself in the clutch the season before, was the centerpiece of the offense and went on to be a finalist for the Heisman Trophy. Cerebral senior Ryan Schmid was the lynchpin of the line at center, and there were future NFL players at each skill position: Keenan Howry, Samie Parker and Jason Willis at receiver, Maurice Morris and Onterrio Smith at running back and Justin Peelle at tight end.

2001 OREGON DUCKS			
September 1	Wisconsin	W	31–28
September 8	Utah	W	24–10
September 22	USC	W	24–22
September 29	at Utah State	W	38–21
October 6	at Arizona	W	63–28
October 13	at California	W	48–7
October 20	Stanford	L	42–49
October 27	at Washington State	W	24–17
November 3	Arizona State	W	42–24
November 10	at UCLA	W	21–20
December 1	Oregon State	W	17–14
January 1	Colorado*	W	38–16

*Fiesta Bowl

On defense, scrappy Eugene native Chris Tetterton defied the odds to start at tackle, while the linebackers were the alliterative trio of David Moretti, Kevin Mitchell and Wesly Mallard (perhaps the most aptly named Duck of them all). Defensive coordinator Nick Aliotti favored an eight-in-the-box defense in those days, and he could afford to with seniors Rashad Bauman and Steve Smith at cornerback.

The season began with some revenge, as the No. 7 Ducks returned a favor from the year before by edging No. 22 Wisconsin on a touch-down plunge by Harrington in the fourth quarter. Oregon went to 2–0 with a win over Utah, then upset USC 24–22 on a last-minute

field goal. Steve Smith intercepted Carson Palmer three times, and Harrington completed 5-of-6 passes on the drive to the game-winning field goal.

The Ducks closed their nonconference schedule by beating Utah State, then thrashed California 48–7. But the perfect season came to an end a week later at home against Stanford. The fifth-ranked Ducks led 42–28 entering the fourth quarter, but the Cardinal used two blocked punts and an interception to score the game's final 21 points, and Harrington was unable to muster his typical magic.

The following week, the Ducks got back on track behind a historic rushing performance.

The thrilling 24–22 win over USC set the stage for more magic to come.

The 2001 Oregon Ducks—11 wins, countless memories

Onterrio Smith, the talented transfer from Tennessee, tore up Washington State for a school-record 285 yards and three touchdowns, while Morris added 138 yards. Oregon then beat Arizona State before scoring on a fourth-quarter pass from Harrington to Josh Line for a one-point win over UCLA.

Up next was the Civil War, a year after Oregon State had crushed Oregon's Rose Bowl hopes. On a cold, rainy night, Howry returned a punt 70 yards to put the Ducks ahead 10–3, and they went on to win 17–14.

Despite being ranked No. 2 in both polls, Oregon was just fourth according to the BCS computers, denying the Ducks a national-title shot. Some might have expected Oregon to fall flat in the Fiesta Bowl, particularly against the powerful running game of the Buffaloes. But Aliotti stacked the box to hold Colorado to 49 rushing yards, and Steve Smith intercepted three passes for the second time that season. Meanwhile, Harrington threw touchdowns to Howry, Parker, Smith and Peelle, while Morris added a dramatic 49-yard scoring run, and the Ducks won 38–16.

In the history of Oregon football, other teams might have been more talented. But with its combination of playmakers and senior leadership, the 2001 Ducks were the most successful team in school history to that point.

Haloti Ngata closes in on Fresno State quarterback Paul Pinegar during the 37–34 thriller.

THE 2005 SEASON

After the disappointment of 2004, the first losing season since Mike Bellotti's tenure began in 1995, expectations weren't particularly high when the 2005 season began. What was then an unknown was that the 2004 juniors had taken the 5–6 record personally and had matured into one of the best groups of leaders in the program's history.

The quarterback in 2005 was an Eastern Oregon cowboy named Kellen Clemens, a tall, athletic passer being asked to direct the team's first season in the spread offense. The running back was a savvy, underrated senior named Terrence Whitehead, with five-star recruit and ace kickoff returner Jonathan Stewart as his backup. Another respected senior, Demetrius Williams, led the receivers, and Enoka Lucas centered a durable line.

The defense was built around mammoth junior tackle Haloti Ngata, who went on to be named a consensus All-American and finalist for the Outland Trophy. Pass rusher Devan Long supplied pressure from one end, and outside linebacker Anthony Trucks led the team in sacks. The secondary included senior cornerbacks Aaron Gipson and Justin Phinisee, and Gipson went on to lead the nation in interceptions.

The 2005 team avoided the disappointing start of the previous year, traveling to Houston and posting a 38–24 victory. In the debut of the spread, Clemens threw for 348 yards and ran for 72 more, and the defense recovered from a slow start to allow only three points after the first quarter. A blowout of Montana followed, and up next was a visit from No. 23 Fresno State.

Like Houston, the Bulldogs also got off to a strong start, taking a 17–0 lead in the second quarter. But once again Clemens led the Ducks back, as he threw three touchdown passes in the second quarter. He added another in the fourth quarter, a nifty catch-and-run by Whitehead, and the Ducks had completed a perfect nonconference run.

2005 Oregon Ducks

Pac-10 play began with a resounding defeat at the hands of USC, with Matt Leinart throwing for 315 yards and Reggie Bush and LenDale White each surpassing 100 on the ground. It was time once again for the 2005 Ducks to rally, and as usual they answered, going the rest of the regular season without a loss.

Clemens threw for 393 yards the next week at Stanford. Backups Dennis Dixon and Brady Leaf were both able to take the field in the blowout victory, the importance of which didn't become clear until weeks later. The No. 25 Ducks went on to beat Arizona State, then moved up five spots in each of the next two polls before beating Washington and then Arizona.

The season nearly took a sickening turn for the worse against the Wildcats when Clemens suffered a broken leg after halftime, and then Dixon was knocked out with a concussion. But Leaf, the younger brother of former Washington State star Ryan Leaf, came on and held his own, while linebacker Brent Haberly, a former walk-on who grew up just south of Eugene, returned a fumble 34 yards for the game-winning touchdown in the fourth quarter.

The Ducks had a bye week before facing No. 23 Cal, allowing them to adjust to the absence of Clemens. Dixon got the start but Leaf also played, and Oregon led 20–10 midway through the third quarter. Cal answered with 10 straight points to tie the game and force overtime, but Leaf threw a touchdown on Oregon's possession, and Cal gained two yards on four plays on its possession, giving Oregon the win.

The next week it was Dixon's turn for dramatics, as he directed the drive to Paul Martinez's game-winning field goal with one second left at Washington State. Then it was time for revenge against Oregon State. Gipson returned an interception for a score, Stewart returned a kickoff for a touchdown for the second time and Dixon threw three touchdown passes in a 56–14 win.

Locked out of the BCS to the chagrin of the program and its fans, the Ducks went to the Holiday Bowl, where they met Oklahoma. Oregon led 7–3 at halftime before the Sooners rallied for 14 points in the third quarter. The Ducks scored with 3:43 left to make it 17–14 and got the ball back with a chance to tie or win, but Leaf threw an interception deep in Oklahoma territory, and the Sooners held on.

It was an unfitting end to a surprisingly strong season for the Ducks, one that was unexpected in many ways considering the trials of the year before. Despite the sour finale, though, this team will always be special to Oregon fans for overcoming so much adversity.

2005 OREGON DUCKS

September 1	at Houston	W	38–24
September 10	Montana	W	47–14
September 17	Fresno State	W	37–34
September 24	USC	L	13–45
October 1	at Stanford	W	44–20
October 8	at Arizona State	W	31–17
October 15	Washington	W	45–21
October 22	at Arizona	W	28–21
November 5	California	W	27–20 ot
November 13	at Washington State	W	34–31
November 19	Oregon State	W	56–14
December 29	Oklahoma*	L	14–17

*Holiday Bowl

Great Moments

GOOD THINGS BRUIN: THE COMEBACK AT UCLA

The 1970 Oregon team was the best of coach Jerry Frei's five seasons in Eugene, and indeed the only one to finish with a winning record. Those Ducks went 6–4–1, which was something of an underachievement given a roster that included Bobby Moore, Bob Newland and sophomore quarterback Dan Fouts. But rather than disappointment, that team will forever be remembered for what it did on October 10 of that fall, in a game at UCLA.

The 1970 Ducks were crippled by injuries, including one to senior quarterback Tom Blanchard. He didn't start that night against the Bruins, but with 4:28 remaining, and the Ducks down 40–21, Frei pulled Fouts and turned to his wounded veteran. The senior found Moore on a 29-yard touchdown pass only 24 seconds later, and the Ducks were within 12.

It's the rare comeback that doesn't include a gift from the opponent, and UCLA provided one with a fumble to give the Ducks the ball right back. Another Blanchard-to-Moore scoring pass made it a five-point game, and Oregon recovered the ensuing onside kick to heighten the dramatics.

The situation turned dire when Blanchard, already dealing with a sore knee, injured his shoulder on the next play. But Fouts, undeterred by the earlier benching, came back in to throw a touchdown pass to Greg Specht in the final minute as the Ducks won 41-40, remarkably erasing a 19-point deficit in the game's final 4:04.

The victory was part of a four-game winning streak that also included a conquest of USC. A tie with Army and rivalry losses to both Washington and Oregon State ruined the team's chances to compete for a league title or bowl berth, but the 1970 Ducks had already secured their legacy with what has been called one of the greatest comebacks in college football history.

THE MUSGRAVE ERA

The years following the 1963 Sun Bowl were lean ones for the Oregon Ducks. They included the final seasons under the legendary Len Casanova, followed by only one winning campaign under the trio of Jerry Frei, Dick Enright and Don Reed. Rich Brooks took the helm for the 1977 season, but he never won more than six games in his first 12 years. That streak ended in 1989, the jumping-off point for Oregon's rise to prominence over the ensuing decade.

Following the departure of Eugene native Chris Miller in 1986, Oregon fans were concerned about the quarterback position. Those questions were answered in resounding fashion in the 1987 opener, as a redshirt freshman named Bill Musgrave directed a 10–7 win in his home state, at Colorado. Along with a veteran defense that included future pros like Anthony Newman and Chris Oldham in the backfield, Musgrave directed a respectable 24–14 loss at

Ohio State the following week. Three more wins followed, including upsets of Washington and USC at
home, and the Ducks found themselves ranked for
the first time since 1970.

With enthusiasm for Oregon football finally
stoked in Eugene, the Ducks got off to a 6–1 start in
1988, only to have Musgrave break his collarbone
in a defeat that began a five-game losing streak to
end the season. But Musgrave was back under
center the next season, a year that saw unprecedented numbers on offense and a return to the
postseason—finally.

Musgrave remained healthy throughout the
1989 season, and the Ducks managed a 7–4 record
in the regular season, their best win total in 25
years. That led to an Independence Bowl berth
against Tulsa, though the Athletic Department
bought 14,000 tickets to lock up the bid and ulti-
mately lost money.

In the game, the Ducks fell behind 24–10, but
Musgrave threw his second touchdown pass late in
the third quarter, then ran for a score to tie it early
in the fourth. A field goal by Gregg McCallum with
3:07 left proved to be the game-winner for a team
that set multiple school scoring records.

The next season, Oregon again went 8–4, with a
loss to Colorado State in the Freedom Bowl. That
season included an upset of Heisman Trophy
winner Ty Detmer and fourth-ranked Brigham
Young in Eugene in a game in which Musgrave
threw for a school-record 489 yards. Not surprisingly, Musgrave graduated as the leading passer in
school history. During his career, a spike in fan
interest led to the addition of skyboxes at Autzen
Stadium and the eventual construction of the
administrative building named for Len Casanova.
That was the opening salvo in an explosion at
Oregon, both in football success and facilities
improvements.

Celebrations were a common occurrence during the Bill Musgrave era.

Pat Johnson's touchdown catch provided the winning points in a thrilling, satisfying 31-28 win over Washington.

DETHRONING THE DAWGS

There is little that brings glee to Oregon fans more than a win over hated Washington. Doing it on the road, against a Husky team ranked No. 6 in the nation, made the 1997 version of the rivalry game one of the most satisfying in school history.

There was no doubt that the 1997 Ducks had talent. But JC transfer Akili Smith couldn't win a battle at quarterback with Jason Maas, and speedy receiver Pat Johnson couldn't hold on to the ball, among other problems.

In Seattle, on November 8, 1997, none of that mattered, as Smith and Johnson connected on one of the biggest plays in school history.

Oregon was 4–4 entering the game, while Washington was 7–1, having won 12 straight Pac-10 games. The Huskies were without their starting quarterback and running back due to injuries, but Marques Tuiasosopo took over under center and finished with 261 yards passing and 95 yards on the ground. He scored on a 42-yard touchdown run, and his 41-yard scoring pass put the Huskies up 28–24 midway through the fourth quarter.

The Ducks took over and drove into Washington territory, but on second-and-10 from the 19-yard line Smith was sacked, setting up third-and-19 from the 29. Rather than proving fatal, the loss of yardage simply set the stage for the Smith-to-Johnson drama.

The wideout, also one of the top sprinters in the Pac-10, raced down the field in single coverage. Smith's pass arrived near the goal line, and Johnson stretched to make the catch. That proved to be the game-winning touchdown, giving Oregon a 31–28 victory.

"I don't know how to explain it, but there's been so many times over the years I could have made a play like that and just didn't have the confidence, but today I finally beat it," Johnson told reporters afterwards. "I started crying I was so happy."

Jubilant Ducks fans could relate after watching their team knock off the hated Dawgs.

THE MAGIC OF AUTZEN STADIUM

It's been called the most intimidating place in the country for an opponent by one national college football writer. Michigan coach Lloyd Carr labeled it the loudest place he had ever played. Eugene's Autzen Stadium may not rival the Big House or the Horseshoe in terms of size, but there's no doubting the homefield advantage it gives Oregon, particularly when well-known nonconference opponents visit.

Decades ago, the Ducks were so bad that opponents would bring them in for home games but rarely honor them with a return trip. Then, in 1982, Notre Dame made the journey West, and the Ducks played the Irish to a 13–13 tie. Oregon came into the game 0–6, and it wasn't the best of Notre Dame teams, but the tone was set for an Autzen revival.

In the ensuing years, Colorado twice came up short in Eugene, and in 1990 the Ducks upset No. 4 Brigham Young. Michigan State was sent packing in 1998, Wisconsin was denied in 2001 and Mississippi State was thrashed in 2002.

On September 20, 2003, Carr and the Wolverines entered Autzen ranked third in the nation. But the No. 22 Ducks were far from awed, jumping out to a 21–6 halftime lead. Michigan insisted on trying to pound away at Oregon with the nation's leading rusher, Chris Perry, who finished with only 26 yards. The Wolverines finally went to the air in the fourth quarter to get within 24–20, but Oregon's Keith Lewis blocked a punt, and Jordan Carey recovered it in the end zone to clinch the victory. John Navarre added a late touchdown pass to make it 31–27, capping his 360-yard day, but Michigan managed only minus-3 rushing yards as a team.

Oregon's string of home victories over teams from Bowl Championship Series conferences came to a resounding halt in the 2004 opener against Indiana, but Autzen Stadium's legend was restored two years later in a controversial win over Oklahoma.

Having lost to the Sooners in Norman, Oklahoma, in 2004 and in the Holiday Bowl the following year, the Ducks were out for revenge when Oklahoma came to Eugene on September 16, 2006. Oregon went ahead 13–6, but the Sooners scored two unanswered touchdowns in the third quarter, then rode tailback Adrian Peterson on the way to a touchdown and two field goals to lead 33–20 with 3:12 left. Fans began

The Rivalries

Some great rivalries have helped define Oregon football and have given fans many of their greatest memories. One of those rivalries just happens to be one of the most heated in all of college football—and it's got the name to match.

THE CIVIL WAR

First played in 1894, the rivalry between the football teams of Oregon and Oregon State soon after became known as the Civil War, a designation that lives on to this day but hasn't always been an accurate characterization of the game's intensity. The history of the series has been marked by violent clashes, both on and off the field, and by games that featured football played at both its best and worst. Oregon dominated play after the turn of the 20th century, but Oregon State asserted itself from the mid-1930s into the 1970s. The Ducks then retook control of the matchup for another 15 years before things evened out, and the home team won every game from 1998 through 2006.

Fittingly, the two schools split the first two matchups; the school known then as Oregon Agricultural College won the inaugural game in 1894, while Oregon gained a measure of revenge the next year. But the tone for the series was really set in 1896, when the schools met twice, once in Eugene and once in Corvallis. Oregon won 2–0 at home and then 12–8 in

Corvallis, the proximity of the games only helping to aggravate tensions that led to Oregon fans being roughed up on the sidelines in the rematch.

Oregon won 38–0 in both 1898 and 1899, and OAC didn't field a team the next two seasons. That 1899 game was among the first—but certainly not the last—in the game's history to feature miserable playing conditions in the rainy Willamette Valley, with the football supposedly getting lost in the mud at one point.

The Beavers won for the first time in a decade in 1907, then had to go another 10 years before winning again. All that losing got under the skin of their fans, who after a 1910 game in Corvallis chased Oregon fans back to the train depot. The fracas was deemed a riot by some and led to the game's cancellation in 1911, followed by neutral site contests the two years after that.

Despite the rivalry's one-sided nature, it was growing in popularity. In 1920, 10,000 fans watched the Civil War, and a crowd of 22,000 braved dreary conditions to take in the 1925 contest. In 1927, the Beavers finally posted their first three-game winning streak in series history, and by then the school was beginning to be known by its present name, Oregon State.

The 1933 Civil War was held in Portland, and 32,000 fans watched the Ducks win to set up a showdown with USC for the conference title and a Rose Bowl berth. Rarely over the next few decades did the matchup have such implications again.

In 1934 the teams engaged in an onfield brawl, and three years later fans got back in the mix. The Beavers won 14–0 in Corvallis,

and on the following Monday a caravan of about 100 cars filled with OSU students drove into Eugene to celebrate. The situation was diffused before growing too rowdy.

That 1937 victory was the second win in a 38-year run of dominance for the Beavers. Between 1936 and 1974, Oregon State won 28 times in the Civil War, lost eight and tied two. In 1962 the Beavers won to keep Oregon from wrapping up a Bluebonnet Bowl berth, and in 1964 Oregon State won in a battle to play in the Rose Bowl. That sparked an eight-game winning streak for OSU, tied for the longest in the series with Oregon's run from 1975 to 1982.

The Ducks also won four straight from 1984 to 1987, and a tie in 1983 helped Oregon go 13 years without losing to OSU. But no glory came from that game on November 19, 1983, which will forever be remembered by Oregonians as "the Toilet Bowl." It was the last scoreless tie in college football history, with wretched weather contributing to 11 turnovers and four missed field goals. In the fourth quarter alone, the Ducks had two interceptions, two fumbles and a missed field goal. Oregon State's longtime radio announcer, Darrell Aune, called it the worst game he ever witnessed.

But recently, play in the series has improved markedly, as have the fortunes of the two programs. Oregon's dramatic victory to clinch a Rose Bowl berth in 1994 sparked a four-game winning streak for the Ducks, but starting in 1998, in the ensuing nine seasons the home team won each game.

"Somewhere down there the Ducks will receive."

—THE PUBLIC ADDRESS ANNOUNCER DURING THE FOG-ENSHROUDED 2005 EDITION OF THE CIVIL WAR

J.J. Birden makes a tough catch against the Beavers.

1980's winning campaign included a 40-21 demolition of Oregon State.

The tide has turned in the UO-UW series.

CONQUERING THE TROJANS

With USC holding a commanding lead in the all-time series history, the Trojans and Ducks aren't considered serious rivals. But in Oregon's rise to national prominence, some of the team's greatest seasons were marked by wins over USC.

In the Ducks' landmark 1994 season, backup quarterback Tony Graziani led a 22–7 win. Four years later, Akili Smith's dramatic 62-yard scramble to a touchdown helped the Ducks to a 17–13 victory. A year after that, the Ducks won a 33–30 triple-overtime thriller in which they tied the game late in regulation on a field goal by Nathan Villegas. But Villegas was injured while celebrating the kick with his holder, quarterback Joey Harrington, and his backup missed a potential game-winner in overtime after the Trojans had earlier missed. After the teams traded touchdowns in the second over-time, USC missed a second field goal, and Oregon's third-string kicker, Josh Frankel, came in to make the winning kick.

The Ducks went on to the first 10-win season in school history in 2000, then won 11 games in 2001, and each season included a win over the Trojans.

Steve Hardin and the Ducks turned a corner with their domination of USC in 1994.

Some of the most satisfying wins in Oregon history have come at the expense of USC.

Talkin' Duck Football

We thought we'd go straight to the source and let some of Oregon's greatest legends—and others with a unique perspective—share their thoughts about Duck football. They put it much better than we could.

*"**Year in, year out,** we weren't the greatest bunch of athletes in the conference, but Cas could get everybody to believe that any time you went out to play you had a chance to win, and we would buy that. Whomever we played, USC or UCLA...we still had a chance to win, and that's the way we would play. He made you believe that that was what you were there to do: win."*

—FORMER UO PLAYER AND ASSISTANT COACH PHIL MCHUGH, ON COACH LEN CASANOVA

*"**The kids believed in him,** that was the big thing. He'd get in the huddle and say, 'Let's get 'em.' Oh, he was a tough kid, tougher than the dickens. His passes wobbled sometimes, but they got there."*

—FORMER UO COACH LEN CASANOVA, ON QUARTERBACK BOB BERRY

"You could ask him to do anything. *Whether you handed him the football or threw him the football, some of the acrobatic, athletic things he showed you on the field were absolutely astounding."*

—FORMER UO COACH JERRY FREI, ON BOBBY MOORE (AHMAD RASHAD)

"Guys who play now have no idea. *Telling people what that week was like is like the stories about parents telling their kids how they had to walk five miles to get the cows and take them to the barn before school. I tell guys how tough it was, and they just don't believe we could have done anything like that. But Coach Brooks said we were going to learn to hit, and we hit every day."*

—CURRENT UO ASSISTANT COACH AND FORMER LINEBACKER DON PELLUM, ON A 1983 BYE WEEK IN WHICH RICH BROOKS REINSTITUTED DAILY DOUBLES

"For some reason, I didn't think the game was over. *Sometimes you've got to get lucky. But the thing about that is, you can't get lucky unless you battle your butt off, and that's what we did today, even when things didn't look good."*

—JOEY HARRINGTON, AFTER 2000'S MIRACULOUS COMEBACK WIN AT ARIZONA STATE

"I was anticipating that pattern, and I took a gamble. *I told myself before the snap that if the receiver went inside, it might be a touchdown or the safety would have to pick him up. But if it was an 'out,' I was going to make the play."*

—KENNY WHEATON, ON HIS 1994 INTERCEPTION RETURN FOR A TOUCHDOWN AGAINST WASHINGTON

Joey Harrington

Mike Bellotti with quarterback Bill Musgrave

"That was the hottest thing this side of hell. *One year we had a fight, and it broke into a free-for-all right on the field."*

—PRE–WORLD WORLD I TAILBACK JOHNNY PARSONS, ON THE CIVIL WAR

"I think I'll stay away from Oregon *from now on. Nothing good has happened for two years now. Oregon just doesn't like me."*

—USC TAILBACK O.J. SIMPSON, AFTER RUSHING FOR ONLY 67 YARDS
AGAINST THE DUCKS DURING HIS HEISMAN CAMPAIGN OF 1968

"This has got to top anything *that ever happened to me. This is about as much guts as a team could show."*

—OREGON COACH JERRY FREI,
AFTER THE DUCKS' DRAMATIC COMEBACK AT UCLA IN 1970

"I'd rather be whipped in a public square *than watch a football game like that."*

—SCHOOL PRESIDENT WILLIAM BOYD,
AFTER OREGON'S 5–0 LOSS TO SAN JOSE STATE IN 1975

"These kids, I don't know how many times *I can say it, but the whole really is greater than the sum of the parts. That right there, that's what Oregon football is all about."*

—MIKE BELLOTTI, AFTER THE 2000 HOLIDAY BOWL WIN OVER TEXAS

"It was ugly. *Even if it had ended 3–0, it would have gone down as one of the ugly games of all time. It will live in infamy."*

—OREGON QUARTERBACK CHRIS MILLER, AFTER THE SCORELESS
TIE IN THE 1983 CIVIL WAR THAT IS REMEMBERED AS THE "TOILET BOWL"

"Playing there is brutal. *They shouldn't lose a game in that place because it is so hard for an opposing team."*

—AN ANONYMOUS OPPOSING COACH,
DESCRIBING AUTZEN STADIUM IN THE 2006 EDITION OF *ATHLON PAC-10 FOOTBALL*

"I saw 10 or 15 fans *walking [out] and I thought, 'They're going to be really mad when we come back and beat them.'"*

—OREGON COACH MIKE BELLOTTI, AFTER THE DUCKS SCORED
TWO TOUCHDOWNS IN THE FINAL 1:12 TO BEAT OKLAHOMA IN 2006

"I like this team. *I think we have the chance to be very good. But I thought last year's team had a chance to be very good, too."*

—OREGON COACH MIKE BELLOTTI PRIOR TO THE 2006 SEASON.
THE DUCKS REWARDED BELLOTTI'S OPTIMISM WITH A STELLAR 10–2
SEASON THAT INCLUDED A 56–14 ROUT OF OREGON STATE

"We're on cloud nine right now. *There is no better feeling than beating the Beavers like that, at home, last game, everything."*

—DEMETRIUS WILLIAMS, FOLLOWING THE DUCKS'
56–14 TROUNCING OF OREGON STATE IN 2005

Dennis Dixon led Oregon's miracle comeback versus Oklahoma in 2006.

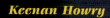
Keenan Howry

"We've been playing football for 105 years. *This is one of the premier events of those 105 years."*

— ATHLETIC DIRECTOR BILL MOOS, ON HARRINGTON BEING A HEISMAN FINALIST IN 2001

"It was a line-drive kick, *and all I had to do was get to the hole. When I broke through, I could hear the crowd, and I looked at the screen to make sure no one would catch me. That play right there, it doesn't get any bigger than that. What a tremendous feeling."*

— KEENAN HOWRY, ON HIS PUNT RETURN FOR A TOUCHDOWN VS. OREGON STATE IN 2001

"He's a tough guy. He was a leader. *He was a guy that lifted this team up, and he's been a great playmaker this year. I thought the marriage of the new [spread] offense with Kellen Clemens was something made in heaven, and it's hard to see him go, and it's hard to see one play take that away. It's difficult. As a coach, I haven't even given in to that feeling yet. I really appreciate Kellen Clemens as a football player and as a quarterback and what he's done for this team."*

— MIKE BELLOTTI, AFTER THE CAREER-ENDING INJURY TO CLEMENS AT ARIZONA IN 2005

"Pride is the word that comes to mind *when I think about what it means to me to be a Duck. I am proud of my associations, acquaintances and friendships that were forged on the rain-soaked AstroTurf of Autzen Stadium."*

— DUCK LEGEND DAN FOUTS

Traditions and Pageantry

What is a college football Saturday without the pageantry? When it comes to the traditions and experiences that make college football so unique—unlike any other sport—the University of Oregon takes a back seat to no other school in the country.

Here's a small sample of what makes Oregon football unique.

GAME DAY

Game day in Eugene often begins before dawn, as recreational vehicles line up outside the parking lots of Autzen Stadium for the right to prime tailgating spots. Both the RVs and the fans inside are decked out in green and yellow, Oregon's school colors since the student body voted to adopt the colors of the state flower—the yellow-blossomed, green-leafed Oregon grape—as their own.

As the day begins, more fans join students in crossing the Willamette River via the Autzen Footbridge, walking from the university's main campus to the athletic facilities. Once on that side of the river, other tailgate gatherings sprout in the parking lots and open fields of nearby businesses, while bars like The Cooler thrive.

Once in the stadium, the 200-member marching band, augmented by a color guard and dance team, leads fans in the alma mater:

Oregon, our Alma Mater, we will

guard thee on and on.

Fellows gather 'round and cheer

her; chant her glory, Oregon.

Roar the praises of her warriors,

sing the glory, Oregon;

On to victory urge the heroes of

our mighty Oregon!

Meanwhile, others are enjoying food, drink and live music in the Moshofsky Center, until the team buses arrive, and players march to the locker room through a phalanx of fans in the indoor practice facility. Then fans settle into their seats in Autzen, where they view a highlight video that always ends with Kenny Wheaton's 1994 interception against Washington, and longtime public address announcer Don Essig reminds them in his booming voice that "it never rains at Autzen Stadium," a beloved if erroneous aspect of Oregon's tradition.

THE MASCOT

Since 1947, Oregon's athletic teams have been represented by Donald Duck, thanks to an agreement between then–athletic director Leo Harris and Walt Disney. The two made a handshake deal on the subject that year, and it was finally put down on paper in 1973.

Prior to that, those trolling the campus in the rainy Willamette Valley were known as Webfoots, in reference to Oregon's early nickname: the Webfoot State. Officials later decided in 1909 that Oregon would be known as the Beaver State, and the beaver was the mascot adopted by OSU. Around then, the University of Oregon's teams began being called the Ducks.

In the 1920s, members of a university fraternity brought a live duck named Puddles to athletic events, a tradition that continued for two decades. The student body officially made Oregon's mascot the Duck with a vote, and the tradition has continued until today.

Kids of all ages love game day at Autzen.

THE IMAGE

With help from Knight and the gurus at Nike, Oregon's marketing strategy under athletic director Bill Moos—along with its success on the football field—boosted the team into the national spotlight.

The first salvo in the marketing blitz was a new set of uniforms unveiled for the 1999 season. The Ducks scrapped their bland yellow helmets and interlocked "UO" logo for metallic green headgear and a new "O" logo, and new color combinations were employed for the jerseys and pants.

But what really caught the nation's attention was a set of all-yellow uniforms unveiled for a game in 2003. Pundits said the Ducks looked like walking highlighters. School officials argued that, lacking a well-known, traditional look like Michigan or Penn State, Oregon's tradition would be one of pushing the envelope. That attitude leapt to new heights in 2006, when another set of new uniforms contained diamond plating on the shoulder pads and included a metallic yellow helmet introduced for that season's Las Vegas Bowl.

Oregon's innovative image was cultivated off the field as well. In 2001 the Athletic Department erected a billboard of Heisman Trophy candidate Joey Harrington in Manhattan, and the next year another was erected to promote the school's agreement to air Oregon football games on an East Coast cable network.

Billboards were also purchased in cities Oregon targeted for recruiting, including one in Los Angeles that riled up an opponent. Three Oregon receivers from the area were displayed on a billboard near USC's campus in 2002. After the Trojans beat the Ducks in Eugene that fall, a trio of Trojans wideouts recreated the billboard on the turf at Autzen Stadium, to the Ducks' chagrin.

Recruits have also been targeted by other innovative means, some since banned by the NCAA, including travel on private jets. The Ducks also have a Hummer truck painted the same metallic green as their helmets, and in 2005 they employed artists to create comic books featuring their recruits as superheroes.

The Ducks look like no other team in football.

Oregon
KWAKI
7

THE FACILITIES

In the facilities arms race that struck college football in recent decades, Oregon has been at the forefront. Beginning with the construction of skyboxes at Autzen Stadium in 1988, the Athletic Department benefited from a construction boom that seemed as if it would never end.

Autzen was built in 1967 for $2.5 million, giving the football team a home after it had previously shared historic Hayward Field with the track squad. A stadium club was added in 1981, and seven years later the department spent over $4 million to add skysuites. Revenue from that project in turn helped fund the $11.8 million Casanova Center, home to administrative offices, in 1991, and the facilities race had begun.

In 1998 the team's $15 million indoor practice facility, the Moshofsky Center, was opened. It was the first such facility on the West Coast and became a big drawing card for warm-weather recruits to the wet state of Oregon.

By that time, Autzen Stadium, once so barren in the lean years of Ducks football, had become a truly formidable place to play. The 2001 team's only loss, to Stanford, ended a 23-game home winning streak, at that time the longest in the nation.

The next season, Oregon unveiled an expanded Autzen, with a seating capacity approaching 60,000, two new levels of skyboxes and a new press box. Since then, Oregon has enhanced its locker room, expanded the weight room and refurbished its athletic treatment center.

THE CONFERENCE

For nearly as long as the Pac-10 Conference and its precursors have existed, Oregon has been a member.

The Ducks' first conference affiliation came about in 1904, when Oregon joined the Northwest Intercollegiate Athletic Association. That league dissolved two years later, and in 1908 the Ducks joined Oregon State, Washington and Washington State in the Northwest Conference. The four would be linked throughout the next century.

Officially, the Pac-10 traces its roots back to December 15, 1915, when the Pacific Coast Conference was formed in Portland, Oregon. Oregon, Washington, Oregon State and California joined, and league play began the following year. In 1917 Washington State joined, and Stanford signed on the year after that.

By 1928 the PCC was up to 10 members, with USC and UCLA among Oregon's new conference mates. The league remained mostly intact, but for an interruption due to World War II, until disbanding in 1959. The four California schools and Washington formed the Athletic Association of Western Universities, and Oregon endured a five-year separation from the league.

That changed in 1964, when the Ducks joined the AAWU. With WSU and OSU also on board, the league changed its name to the Pacific-8 Conference in 1968, and a decade later Arizona and Arizona State were admitted. The Pac-10 was complete, with Oregon considered one of its charter members.

Onterrio Smith (top); Bill Musgrave (right)

Danny O'Neil is Oregon's career passing leader in several categories.

Facts and Figures

CAREER STATISTICAL LEADERS

- Rushes: 811, Derek Loville, 1986–1989
- Rushing Yards: 3,296, Derek Loville, 1986–1989
- Passing Attempts: 1,132, Danny O'Neil, 1991–1994
- Completions: 636, Danny O'Neil, 1991–1994
- Passing Yardage: 8,343, Bill Musgrave, 1987–1990
- Touchdown Passes: 62, Danny O'Neil, 1991–1994
- Receptions: 178, Samie Parker, 2000–2003
- Receiving Yardage: 2,761, Samie Parker, 2000–2003
- Receiving Touchdowns: 24, Keenan Howry, 1999–2002; Cristin McLemore, 1992–1995
- Total Offense: 8,140, Bill Musgrave, 1987–1990
- Punt Return Average: 14.7, Cliff Hicks, 1985–1987
- Kickoff Return Average: 34.1, Woodley Lewis, 1948–1949
- Punting Average: 42.9, Mike Preacher, 1984–1986
- Scoring: 323, Jared Siegel, 2001–2004
- Interceptions: 18, George Shaw, 1951–1954
- Tackles: 433, Tom Graham, 1969–1971
- Sacks: 29, Ernest Jones, 1990–1993
- Tackles for Loss: 48, Devan Long, 2002–2005

1994 Rose Bo

ALL-TIME BOWL GAME SCORES

Bowl	Date	Result
Rose	January 1, 1917	Oregon 14, Pennsylvania 0
Rose	January 1, 1920	Harvard 7, Oregon 6
Cotton	January 1, 1949	SMU 21, Oregon 13
Rose	January 1, 1958	Ohio State 10, Oregon 7
Liberty	December 17, 1960	Penn State 41, Oregon 12
Sun	December 31, 1963	Oregon 21, SMU 14
Independence	December 16, 1989	Oregon 27, Tulsa 24
Freedom	December 29, 1990	Colorado State 32, Oregon 31
Independence	December 31, 1992	Wake Forest 39, Oregon 35
Rose	January 2, 1995	Penn State 38, Oregon 20
Cotton	January 1, 1996	Colorado 38, Oregon 6
Las Vegas	December 20, 1997	Oregon 41, Air Force 13
Aloha	December 25, 1998	Colorado 51, Oregon 43
Sun	December 31, 1999	Oregon 24, Minnesota 20
Holiday	December 29, 2000	Oregon 35, Texas 30
Fiesta	January 1, 2002	Oregon 38, Colorado 16
Seattle	December 30, 2002	Wake Forest 38, Oregon 17
Sun	December 31, 2003	Minnesota 31, Oregon 30
Holiday	December 29, 2005	Oklahoma 17, Oregon 14
Las Vegas	December 21, 2006	BYU 38, Oregon 8

Overall

Won 7, Lost 13, Tied 0

DUCKS IN THE COLLEGE FOOTBALL HALL OF FAME

Name	Position	Years	Inducted
John Beckett	Tackle	1913–1916	1972
Hugo Bezdek	Coach	1906, 1913–1917	1954
Len Casanova	Coach	1951–1966	1977
Johnny Kitzmiller	Halfback	1928–1930	1969
Mel Renfro	Halfback	1961–1963	1986
Norm Van Brocklin	Quarterback	1946–1948	1966

DUCKS IN THE PRO FOOTBALL HALL OF FAME

Dan Fouts, QB

Inducted 1993

San Diego Chargers, 1973–1987

- Six-time Pro Bowler, three-time All-Pro
- Third player ever to pass for more than 40,000 yards
- AFC Player of the Year, 1979, 1982
- Career: 43,040 yards passing, 254 touchdowns

Alphonse Leemans, HB/FB

Inducted 1978

New York Giants, 1936–1943

- All-NFL, 1936, 1939
- Led NFL rushers as a rookie, 1936
- Second-team All-NFL five times
- Career: 3,132 yards rushing, 2,318 yards passing, 422 yards receiving

Mel Renfro, CB/S

Inducted 1996

Dallas Cowboys, 1964–1977

- Earned Pro Bowl berths his first 10 seasons in the league
- All-Pro five times, All-Conference seven times
- Led the NFL in interceptions in 1969; punt and kickoff returns, 1964
- Career: 52 interceptions

Norm Van Brocklin, QB

Inducted 1971

Los Angeles Rams, 1949–1957

Philadelphia Eagles, 1958–1960

- Led NFL in passing three years, punting twice
- 73-yard pass gave Rams the 1951 title
- Led Eagles to the 1960 NFL Championship
- NFL MVP, 1960
- Nine-time Pro Bowler
- Career: 23,611 yards passing, 173 touchdowns

Dave Wilcox, LB

Inducted 2000

San Francisco 49ers, 1964–1974

- All-NFL five times, second-team All-NFL three times
- Seven-time Pro Bowler
- Considered by many the finest outside linebacker of his era
- Nicknamed "the Intimidator"

Chad Cota

OREGON'S FIRST-TEAM ALL-AMERICANS

Shy Huntington, QB, 1916
George Christensen, TE, 1931
Mike Mikulak, HB, 1933
Raymond Morse, TE, 1934
Jake Leight, HB, 1945
Norm Van Brocklin, QB, 1948
George Shaw, QB, 1954
Steve Barnett, T, 1961, 1962
Mel Renfro, HB, 1962, 1963
Bob Berry, QB, 1964
Jim Smith, DB, 1967
Bob Newland, WR, 1970
Bobby Moore, RB, 1971
Tom Drougas, OT, 1971
Gary Zimmerman, G, 1983
Lew Barnes, WR, 1985
Chris Oldham, CB, 1989
Herman O'Berry, CB, 1994
Chad Cota, SS, 1994
Alex Molden, CB, 1995
Haloti Ngata, DL, 2005